Polo 1975-77 Autobook

By Kenneth Ball
Associate Member, Guild of Motoring Writers
and the Autobooks Team of Technical Writers

Volkswagen Polo 1975-77
Volkswagen Polo L 1975-76
Volkswagen Polo N 1976-77
Volkswagen Polo LS 1976-77

Autobooks

Autobooks Ltd. Golden Lane Brighton BN1 2QJ England

The AUTOBOOK series of Workshop Manuals is the largest in the world and covers the majority of British and Continental motor cars, as well as the majority of Japanese and Australian models.

Whilst every care has been taken to ensure correctness of information it is obviously not possible to guarantee complete freedom from errors or to accept liability arising from such errors or omissions.

CONTENTS

ISBN 0 85147 674 0

First Edition   1976
Second Edition, fully revised   1977

© Autobooks Ltd 1977

874

Printed and bound in Brighton England for Autobooks Ltd by G. Beard & Son Ltd

B

ACKNOWLEDGEMENT

My thanks are due to Volkswagen (GB) Limited for their unstinted co-operation and also for supplying data and illustrations.

Considerable assistance has also been given by owners, who have discussed their cars in detail, and I would like to express my gratitude for this invaluable advice and help.

Kenneth Ball
Associate Member, Guild of Motoring Writers
Ditchling Sussex England.

INTRODUCTION

This do-it-yourself Workshop Manual has been specially written for the owner who wishes to maintain his vehicle in first class condition and to carry out the bulk of his own servicing and repairs. Considerable savings on garage charges can be made, and one can drive in safety and confidence knowing the work has been done properly.

Comprehensive step-by-step instructions and illustrations are given on most dismantling, overhauling and assembling operations. Certain assemblies require the use of expensive special tools, the purchase of which would be unjustified. In these cases information is included but the reader is recommended to hand the unit to the agent for attention.

Throughout the Manual hints and tips are included which will be found invaluable, and there is an easy to follow fault diagnosis at the end of each chapter.

Whilst every care has been taken to ensure correctness of information it is obviously not possible to guarantee complete freedom from errors or omissions or to accept liability arising from such errors or omissions.

Instructions may refer to the righthand or lefthand sides of the vehicle or the components. These are the same as the righthand or lefthand of an observer standing behind the vehicle and looking forward.

CHAPTER 1

THE ENGINE

1:1 Description

The engine is an in-line, four-cylinder, single overhead camshaft unit with crossflow induction and exhaust. The unit is transversely mounted and inclined slightly forwards in the engine compartment. The camshaft is driven by a toothed belt instead of the more conventional timing chain. This belt also drives the water pump by means of an auxiliary sprocket, the pump mounting position being adjustable to allow belt tension to be correctly set. The distributor is mounted on the cylinder head and driven by a dog engaging with the end of the camshaft. A special eccentric on the camshaft drives the fuel pump, which is also mounted on the cylinder head.

The valves are set in line along the cylinder head and operated from the camshaft by means of finger type rockers. Valve clearance adjustment is provided for at the ball head screws on which the rockers are mounted, the screws being turned in or out to alter the clearance between rockers and cams.

The cylinder block is integral with the upper half of the crankcase, the lower half of which is formed by the pressed steel sump. The light-alloy pistons are each provided with two compression rings and one oil control ring. Gudgeon pins are a light press fit in pistons and

connecting rods and are retained by means of circlips.

The two versions of the engine, 900cc and 1100cc, differ in stroke dimension, sharing the same bore size.

The five bearing counterbalanced crankshaft is a special steel casting. Crankshaft end thrust is taken by the flanged centre bearing. Both main and big-end bearings are provided with renewable shell type inserts.

The eccentric gear-type oil pump is driven directly from the end of the crankshaft. Pressure oil is fully filtered before being passed to the lubrication points in the engine.

1:2 Removing and refitting the engine

The normal operations of decarbonising and servicing the cylinder head can be carried out without the need for engine removal, as can the majority of engine servicing procedures. A major overhaul, however, can only be satisfactorily carried out with the engine removed and transferred to the bench. For some overhaul work, certain special tools are essential and the owner would be well advised to check on the availability of these factory tools or suitable substitutes before tackling the items involved. Note also that the attachment screws and bolts for certain components must be turned by means of a special hexagon (Allen) key of the correct size.

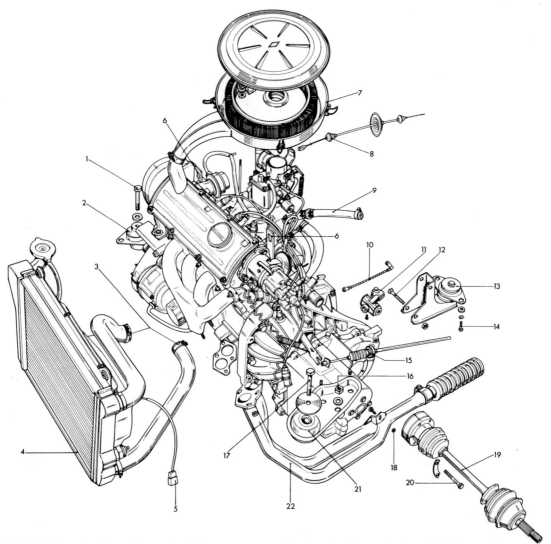

FIG 1:1 Layout of the engine and ancilliary components, showing the items to be detached before engine removal

Key to Fig 1:1 1 Righthand mounting bolt   2 Righthand engine mounting   3 Radiator hoses   4 Radiator   5 Fan motor connection   6 Engine lifting lugs   7 Air cleaner assembly   8 Accelerator cable   9 Heater hose   10 Earth strap   11 Selector rod connector   12 Bolt   13 Righthand rear engine bearing   14 Screw   15 Clutch cable   16 Nut   17 Lefthand bearing bolt   18 Exhaust pipe mounting nut   19 Driveshaft   20 Flange bolt   21 Lefthand engine mounting   22 Exhaust pipe

If the operator is not a skilled automobile engineer, it is suggested that he will find much useful information in **Hints on Maintenance and Overhaul** at the end of this manual and that he read it before starting work. It must be stressed that the lifting equipment used to remove the engine from the car should be sound, firmly based and not likely to collapse under the weight it will be supporting. The engine and transmission are removed as a unit, then the transmission separated from the engine.

Removal:

The bonnet should be propped in the fully open position, not removed. Drain the engine oil. Refer to

FIG 1:1. Slacken the hose clips and detach hoses 3 from the engine. Allow the coolant to drain through the bottom hose, collecting the coolant in a clean container if it is to be re-used. Pull off the cooling fan motor connection 5, then remove the fixing bolts and lift out radiator assembly 4.

Release the spring clips and remove the cover and filter element, then remove the air cleaner body 7. Unscrew the accelerator cable 8 at the carburetter, then disconnect the cable from the holder by pressing the clips together as shown in **FIG 1:2**. Disconnect the choke cable at the carburetter and the fuel pipe at the fuel pump.

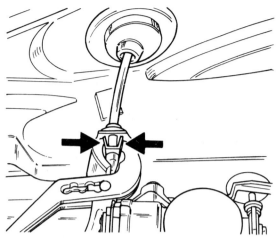

FIG 1:2   Carburetter cable clips

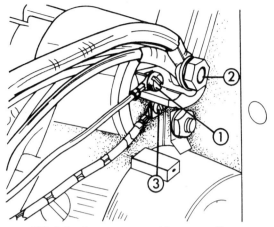

FIG 1:3   Starter motor wiring connections

Refer to **FIG 1:1**. Disconnect heater hoses 9 from the body connections and earth strap 10 from the transmission. Slacken the adjuster nut on clutch cable 15 and disconnect the cable from the release lever. Detach the cable from the fitting on the transmission. Disconnect the battery earth cable, then disconnect the leads from the starter motor at points 1, 2 and 3 in **FIG 1:3**. Terminal 1 was only used in earlier cars fitted with a series resistance in the ignition coil circuit. Disconnect the speedometer cable at the transmission.

Disconnect the exhaust pipe 22 (see **FIG 1:1**) at the manifold flange and transmission connection. Tie the exhaust pipe away from the work area so that the pipe is not unduly strained. Disconnect both lefthand and righthand drive shafts 19 at their inner flanges, referring to **Chapter 7** for detailed instructions. Support the inner ends of the shafts by tying to the body to prevent damage.

Disconnect the central HT lead and the LT lead that connects to the distributor from the coil. Disconnect the alternator wiring.

Disconnect the gear selector rod from connector 11, using tool VW 114 or similar as shown in **FIG 1:4**. Check that all wiring and hoses have been disconnected from the engine assembly.

Securely attach the lifting equipment to engine lifting lugs 6, then raise slightly to take the weight of engine and transmission unit. Unscrew and remove rear engine mounting 13, as shown in **FIG 1:5**. Remove centre bolt 1 from righthand engine mounting 2, as shown in **FIG 1:6**. The righthand engine mounting itself remains in position. Remove the lefthand engine mounting 21, as shown in **FIG 1:7**. Lift the engine and transmission assembly from the engine compartment as shown in **FIG 1:8**.

Refitting:

Refitting the engine and transmission assembly to the car is basically a reversal of the removal procedure, noting the following points:

Position righthand engine bearing screw and install lefthand engine bearing, but do not fully tighten the fixings. Have an assistant load the car to compress the road springs, at a point level with the rear of the engine

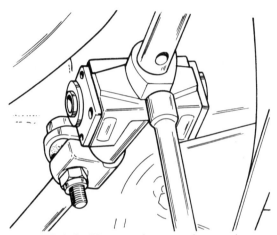

FIG 1:4   Disconnecting gear selector rod

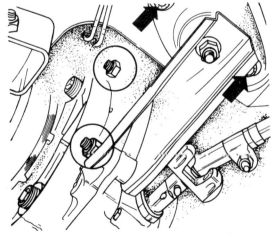

FIG 1:5   Rear engine mounting removal

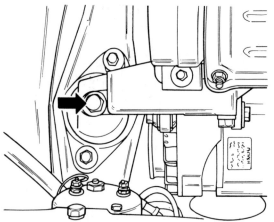

FIG 1:6 Righthand engine mounting bolt removal

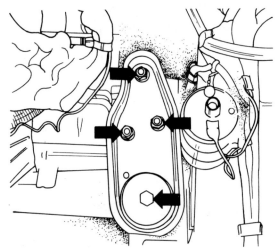

FIG 1:7 Lefthand engine mounting removal

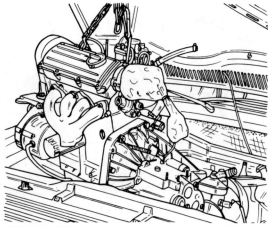

FIG 1:8 Lifting engine and transmission from vehicle

compartment, then attach the drive shafts to the transmission flanges. Do not fully tighten the fixing bolts. Install the rear engine mounting, then tighten all engine mounting and drive shaft fixings, observing the following torque wrench settings (see **FIG 1:1**). Bolt 1 40Nm (29lb ft); bolt 12, 42Nm (30lb ft); bolt 14, 30Nm (21.5lb ft); bolt 17, 55Nm (39.5lb ft); and bolts 20, 40Nm (29lb ft).

When refitting earth strap 10 to the transmission, make sure that the mating surfaces of the connector and transmission case are clean and dry. Use a new manifold gasket when reconnecting the exhaust pipe and tighten the flange nuts and support nut 18 to 25Nm (18lb ft).

When refitting the accelerator cable, have an assistant depress the accelerator pedal fully and hold it there. Guide the cable into the clamping screw, then move the throttle lever on the carburetter to the full throttle position and tighten the clamping screw. Release the accelerator pedal.

On completion, check clutch cable adjustment as described in **Chapter 5**, adjust the gear selector mechanism as described in **Chapter 6** and refill and bleed the cooling system as described in **Chapter 4**. Check for a smooth idle when the engine is warmed up to normal operating temperature, adjusting the carburetter if necessary as described in **Chapter 2**. Check the engine oil level and top up if necessary.

1:3 Timing belt removal

Timing belt installation details are shown in **FIG 1:9**. Remove cover 7, then slacken and remove alternator drive belt 4 as described in **Chapter 11**. Turn the engine by means of a spanner on crankshaft pulley bolt 6, or by pushing the car forwards in top gear, until the timing marks on crankshaft and camshaft sprocket are correctly aligned with the pointers as shown in **FIG 1:10**.

Slightly slacken the mounting bolts for water pump 2, then move the water pump with the screwdriver as shown in **FIG 1:11** until the toothed belt is slack enough to be removed from the pulleys.

Unless the cylinder head is completely removed, the crankshaft and camshaft must not be turned independently, otherwise the valves may contact the pistons and cause internal damage.

To refit the timing belt, check to make sure that the camshaft and crankshaft timing marks are correctly aligned as shown in **FIG 1:10**, then refit the belt over the pulleys. Set the belt to the correct tension as described next.

Checking timing belt tension:

Timing belt tension should be checked and correctly set after any servicing operation involving slackening of the belt and on a regular basis as part of routine maintenance.

To check belt tension, refer to **FIG 1:9** and remove cover 7. When correctly tensioned, the toothed belt must just barely turn 90° when twisted with thumb and index finger. If tension is incorrect, turn the engine until the timing marks on camshaft and crankshaft pulleys are correctly aligned as shown in **FIG 1:10**, in case the timing belt should slip and one of the pulleys turn in relation to the other during the tensioning procedure.

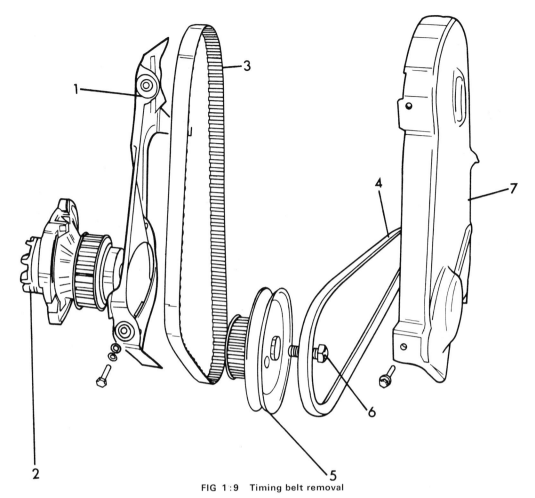

FIG 1:9 Timing belt removal

Key to Fig 1:9 1 Inner cover 2 Water pump 3 Toothed belt 4 Alternator drive belt 5 Crankshaft pulley 6 Pulley bolt 7 Outer cover

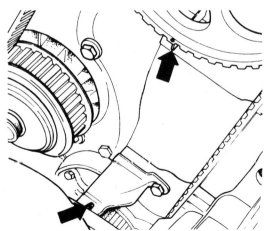

FIG 1:10 Correct alignment of camshaft and crankshaft timing marks

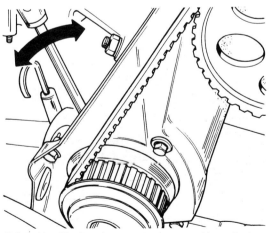

FIG 1:11 Moving the water pump assembly to slacken or tighten toothed belt

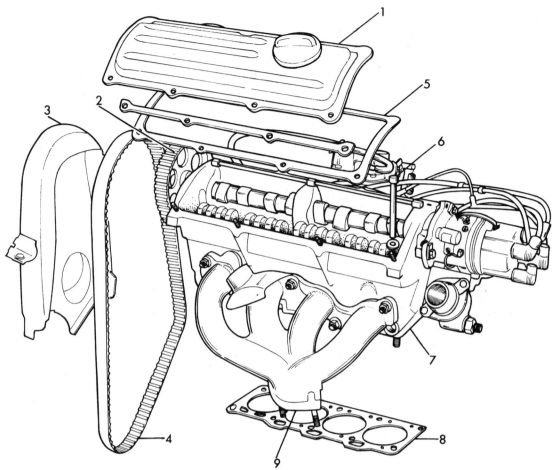

FIG 1:12 Cylinder head removal

Key to Fig 1:12   1 Camshaft cover   2 Camshaft pulley   3 Belt cover   4 Toothed belt   5 Gasket   6 Cylinder head bolt
7 Cylinder head   8 Head gasket   9 Exhaust manifold

FIG 1:13 Cylinder head bolt tightening sequence.
Loosen in the reverse order

Slacken the bolts securing the water pump assembly to the cylinder block. Use a screwdriver to move the water pump on its mountings as shown in **FIG 1:11**. Lever the water pump outwards until belt tension is correct, then fully tighten the water pump mountings and recheck the tension. Note that the pulleys may move very slightly from their set positions during the tightening procedure, but this will not affect the engine timing. On completion, refit the front cover. If the alternator drive belt was removed, refit and set to the correct tension as described in **Chapter 11**.

If the belt is found to be worn or damaged during any of the regular inspections, it should be discarded and a new belt obtained and fitted.

1:4 Removing and refitting cylinder head

The cylinder head can be removed, serviced and refitted without the need for engine removal.

Removal:

Drain the cooling system as described in **Chapter 4**. Release the spring clips and remove the air cleaner cover

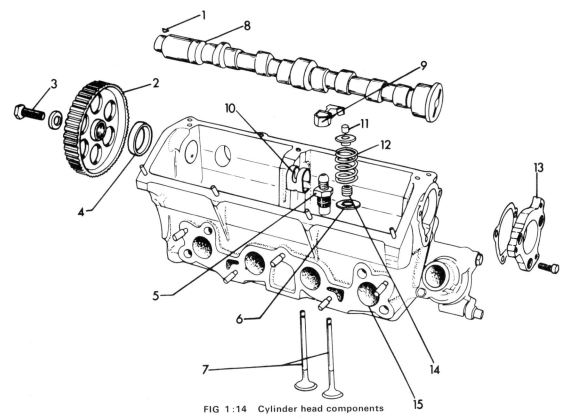

FIG 1 :14 Cylinder head components

Key to Fig 1 :14   1 Key   2 Camshaft pulley   3 Pulley bolt   4 Seal   5 Ballhead screw   6 Lower spring cap   7 Inlet and exhaust valves   8 Camshaft   9 Rocker arm   10 Spring clamp   11 Collets   12 Valve spring   13 Distributor flange 14 Valve stem seal   15 Cylinder head

and filter element, then remove the complete air cleaner body (see **FIG 1 :1**). Disconnect the exhaust pipe from the manifold flange, collecting the gasket (see **FIG 1 :1**). Remove the accelerator cable from the carburetter and bracket as described in **Section 1 :2** and disconnect the choke cable from the carburetter. Disconnect all hoses and electrical wiring from the cylinder head connections.

If cylinder head overhaul and decarbonising is to be carried out, remove the distributor as described in **Chapter 3** and remove the sparking plugs.

Remove the timing belt as described in **Section 1 :3**. Refer to **FIG 1 :12** and remove the nuts securing camshaft cover 1. Lift off the camshaft cover and carefully remove gasket 5. Slacken cylinder head bolts 6 in the reverse order to that shown in **FIG 1 :13**, then fully unscrew and remove the bolts. Lift off cylinder head 7, pulling against the exhaust manifold to loosen the head from the gasket if it sticks in position. Remove and discard head gasket 8.

Refitting:

Carefully clean the mating surfaces of cylinder head and cylinder block, avoiding the use of sharp tools which could scratch the surfaces. Refer to **FIG 1 :12** and fit a new head gasket 8 to the cylinder block, making sure that the gasket is the correct way up by checking that

each hole in the gasket matches the bore in the cylinder block surface. Fit the cylinder head into position and install the head bolts finger tight. Tighten the bolts a little at a time in the order shown in **FIG 1 :13** to a final torque of 65Nm (47lb ft) cold or 75Nm (54lb ft) hot.

Refit the remaining components in the reverse order of removal, using a new gasket between exhaust manifold and exhaust pipe flange. Renew the camshaft cover gasket if the original is damaged or leaking. Refit and correctly tension the toothed belt as described in **Section 1 :3**. On completion, refill and bleed the cooling system as described in **Chapter 4** and, if necessary, carry out the engine idling speed adjustments as described in **Chapter 2**. After the car has been driven for a distance of approximately 500km (300 miles), the cylinder head bolts should be retightened to the correct torque when the engine is at normal operating temperature. To do this, remove the camshaft cover then slacken each bolt through approximately 30° then tighten to the correct torque in the order shown in **FIG 1 :13**.

1 :5 Servicing head, valves and camshaft

Remove the cylinder head as described in **Section 1 :4** and transfer it to the bench, taking care not to damage the joint surfaces or ancillary components.

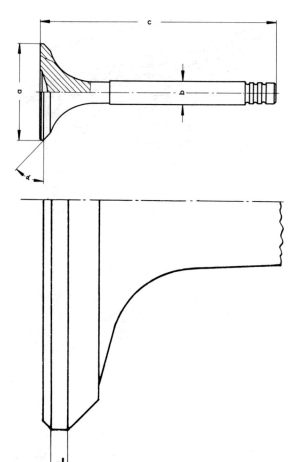

FIG 1:15 Correct machining dimensions for inlet valves. Exhaust valves must not be machined

Key to Fig 1:15 a 31.6mm inlet, 28.1mm exhaust b 7.97mm inlet, 7.95mm exhaust c 104mm, inlet and exhaust d 0.5mm minimum (inlet) Seat angle 45°

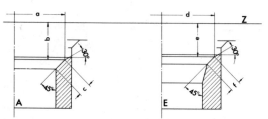

FIG 1:16 Correct machining dimensions for cylinder head valve seat inserts

Key to Fig 1:16 Z Bottom edge of cylinder head 30° correction angle, top 45° valve seat angle A Exhaust valve a 26.5mm diameter b 9.15mm c 2.40mm E Inlet valve d 30.0mm diameter e 8.85mm f 2.00mm

Dismantling:

Remove the exhaust manifold, inlet manifold with carburetter, and fuel pump assembly from the cylinder head. If not previously removed, detach the distributor as described in **Chapter 3**. If necessary, remove thermostat housing assembly as shown in **Chapter 4, FIG 4:6**.

Refer to **FIG 1:14**. Turn the camshaft so that each camshaft lobe in turn is pointing away from its valve assembly, then carefully remove spring clamps 10. Tighten ball head screws 5 several turns, then detach rocker arms 9. Keep all valve gear components in the correct order for refitting in their original positions if they are not to be renewed. Remove distributor flange 13 with gasket. Unscrew bolt 3 and remove camshaft pulley 2, collecting key 1. If camshaft seal 4 is in good condition, the camshaft can be carefully removed leaving the seal in position, taking care not to damage the seal lips. If the seal is to be renewed, it can be removed without the need for camshaft removal using tool 2002. Fit a new seal and drive it fully home, keeping it square to the bore. The special tool for seal installation is 10-203.

Withdraw the camshaft from the distributor end of the cylinder head. Use a suitable valve spring compressor to remove the valve gear from the cylinder head. With the spring compressed, remove the split taper collets 11, then remove the compressor tool and collect the valve 7, spring 12, seal 14 and the spring caps (see **FIG 1:14**). Keep all valve gear components in the correct order for refitting in their original positions if they are not to be renewed. Discard the valve shaft seals as new ones must be fitted during reassembly.

Valves:

When the valves have been cleaned of carbon deposits, they must be inspected for serviceability. Valves with bent stems or badly burned heads must be renewed. Inlet valves that are pitted can be recut at a service station, but if they are too far gone for this remedial treatment new valves will be required. The correct machining dimensions for inlet valves are shown in **FIG 1:15**. Exhaust valves that are in poor condition must be renewed as no machining is permissible. All valves that are in serviceable condition can be ground to their seats as described later.

Valve seat inserts:

Valve seat inserts that are pitted or burned must be refaced at a service station. The correct machining angles and dimensions for valve seat inserts are shown in **FIG 1:16**. If any valve seat insert is too worn or damaged for this remedial treatment to be effective, the cylinder head assembly must be renewed as it is not possible to renew seat inserts separately. If the valve seat inserts are serviceable, they should be ground to the valves as described later.

Valve guides:

Any valve guide worn beyond the tolerance limit or badly scored, will dictate renewal of the cylinder head assembly as it is not possible to renew valve guides separately. Valve guide wear should be checked by means of a dial gauge mounted on the cylinder head as

FIG 1:17   Checking valve stem clearance in guide

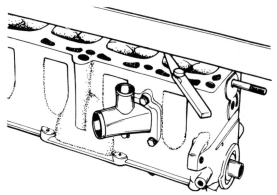

FIG 1:18   Checking cylinder head for distortion

shown in **FIG 1:17**. It is essential to use a new valve of the correct type to obtain accurate measurements. Fit the new valve into the guide as shown and move it away from the gauge by hand. Zero the gauge against the valve head, then push the valve towards the gauge and check the reading. The wear limits are 1.0mm for inlet valves, 1.3mm for exhaust valves.

Valve springs:

Carefully inspect the valve springs and renew any that are found damaged or distorted. Test all valve springs that appear in good condition by comparing their efficiency with that of new springs. To do this, insert both the old and new springs end to end with a metal plate between them into the jaws of a vice or under a press. If the old spring is weakened, it will close up first when pressure is applied. Take care that the springs do not fly out of the vice or press under pressure. Any spring which is shorter or weaker than a new spring should be renewed.

Cylinder head:

Carefully clean the cylinder head and make sure that all oil and water passages are clear. Check the mating surface for flatness, using a straightedge and feeler gauges as shown in **FIG 1:18**. It should not be possible to fit a 0.1mm feeler between straightedge and cylinder head surface at any point. If the mating surface is distorted beyond the limit stated, the head should be refaced at a service station. If the distortion is too serious for this remedial work to be carried out satisfactorily, or if the head is cracked or otherwise damaged, a new cylinder head should be fitted.

Decarbonising and valve grinding:

Avoid the use of sharp tools which could damage the cylinder head or piston surfaces. Remove all traces of carbon deposits from the combustion chambers, inlet and exhaust ports and joint faces. If the pistons have not been removed and cleaned during previous engine dismantling, plug the oilways and waterways in the top surface of the cylinder block with pieces of rag to prevent the entry of dirt, then clean the carbon from the piston crowns.

To grind-in valves, use medium grade carborundum paste unless the seats are in very good condition, when fine grade paste can be used at once. A light spring under the valve head will assist in the operation and allow the valve to be lifted from its seat without releasing the

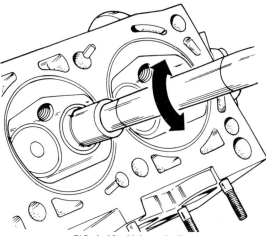

FIG 1:19   Valve grinding

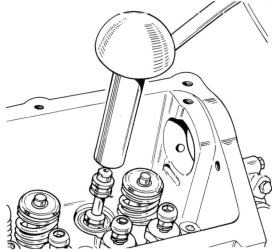

FIG 1:20   Installing valve stem seals

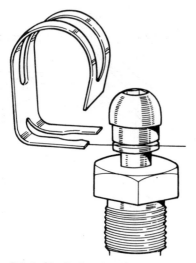

FIG 1:21 Spring clamp installation

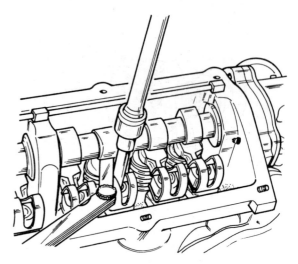

FIG 1:22 Valve clearance adjustment

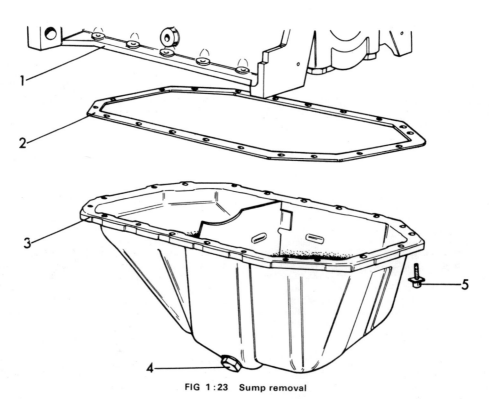

FIG 1:23 Sump removal

Key to Fig 1:23   1 Crankcase   2 Gasket   3 Sump   4 Drain plug   5 Screw

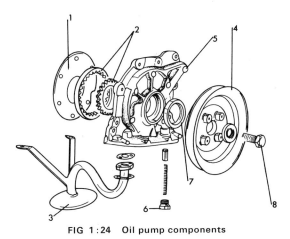

FIG 1:24 Oil pump components

Key to Fig 1:24 1 Pump cover 2 Pump gears 3 Oil strainer 4 Crankshaft pulley 5 Pump housing 6 Pressure relief valve 7 Seal 8 Pulley bolt

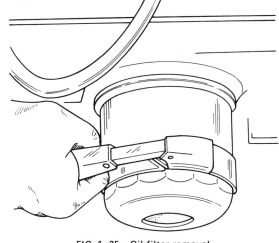

FIG 1:25 Oil filter removal

grinding tool. Use a suction cup tool and grind with a semi-rotary movement (see **FIG 1:19**). Allow the valve to rise off its seat occasionally by pressure of the spring under the head, then turn to a new position before resuming the grinding procedure. Use paste sparingly. When both seats have a smooth matt grey finish, clean away every trace of grinding paste from port and valve.

Camshaft and rockers:

Examine the rockers for excessive wear of the working surfaces and inspect for cracks or other damage. Examine the ballhead screws for excessive wear of the rocker bearing surfaces and for wear or damage of the threads. Renew any faulty components.

Inspect the working surfaces of camshaft lobes and journals for signs of wear, damage or seizure. Mount the camshaft between pivot centres or in V-blocks and check the runout at the centre bearing position, using a dial gauge. Runout must not exceed 0.02mm. Fit the camshaft to the cylinder head and install the distributor flange with gasket, then check camshaft axial play using a dial gauge. Axial play should not exceed 0.24mm. Excessive play will dictate renewal of worn components.

Check the camshaft pulley and the pulleys on crankshaft and water pump for worn or broken teeth. Thoroughly clean the pulleys to remove any dirt from between the teeth. Do not use metal tools or a wire brush for cleaning purposes, as this may damage the surfaces.

Reassembly:

This is a reversal of the dismantling procedure, noting the following points:

Use a new camshaft oil seal if the original is not in perfect condition, and use new gaskets throughout. Lubricate camshaft journals and lobes and valve stems with engine oil.

Carefully fit new seals to the valve stems as shown in **FIG 1:20**. If possible, this operation should be carried out using special tool 10-204 to avoid damage to the seals. Make sure that the spring clamps are fitted

correctly to the ballhead screws as shown in **FIG 1:21**. Turn the camshaft until the pulley mark is as shown in **FIG 1:10** and both camshaft lobes for No. 1 (pulley end) cylinder are away from the valves.

After refitting the cylinder head as described in **Section 1:4**, adjust the valve clearances as described next.

1:6 Valve clearance adjustment

The correct adjustment of valve clearances is important as they affect engine timing and performance considerably. Excessive clearance will reduce valve lift and opening duration and reduce engine performance, causing excessive wear on the valve gear components and noisy operation. Insufficient or zero clearance will again affect engine timing and, in some circumstances, can hold the valve clear of its seat. This will result in much reduced performance due to lost compression and the possibility of burned valves and seats. Valve clearances should be checked at the intervals recommended in the owner's handbook as routine maintenance and, additionally, whenever the cylinder head has been serviced.

Final adjustment should be made when the cylinder head is warm (coolant temperature at about 35°C), the correct clearances under these conditions being 0.20mm for inlet valves and 0.30mm for exhaust valves. However, if the cylinder head has been overhauled the valve clearance should first be set to 0.15mm for inlet valves and 0.25mm for exhaust valves with the engine cold. This allows the engine to be started and safely run until it reaches approximately 35°C, when final adjustment should be carried out to the figures given previously. Counting from the camshaft drive belt (righthand) end of the engine, inlet valves are numbers 1, 3, 5 and 7, and exhaust valves numbers 2, 4, 6 and 8.

Run the engine until it is at the correct temperature, then switch off and remove the camshaft cover (see **FIG 1:12**). Turn the engine until both valves of one cylinder are in the closed position, this being when the cam lobes for that cylinder point away from the valves by

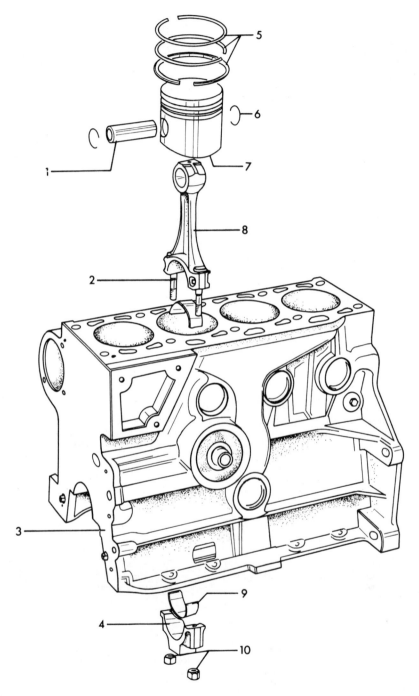

FIG 1:26 Piston and connecting rod removal

Key to Fig 1:26   1 Gudgeon pin   2 Connecting rod bolt   3 Cylinder block   4 Connecting rod cap   5 Piston rings
6 Circlip   7 Piston   8 Connecting rod   9 Bearing shell   10 Nuts

equal amounts. Turn the engine by means of a spanner on the crankshaft pulley bolt or by selecting top gear and pushing the car forwards. Never attempt to turn the camshaft pulley or its bolt as this would overload and damage the toothed timing belt.

Check the clearance between the base of the cam lobe and the upper surface of the rocker with feeler gauge, as shown in **FIG 1 : 22**. A feeler of the correct thickness should slide in the gap with a slight drag, being neither tight nor loose. If the clearance is incorrect, turn the ball end screw with a suitable hexagon key, such as tool V.150. Turn anticlockwise to decrease clearance, clockwise to increase. Repeat the operation on the second valve of the pair, then repeat the entire operation at each remaining pair of valves.

On completion, refit the camshaft cover, using a new gasket if the original is not in perfect condition.

1 : 7 Sump removal

The sump can be removed with the engine in situ. Refer to **FIG 1 : 23**. Place a suitable container beneath the sump to catch the oil then remove drain plug 4. When the oil has drained fully, refit the plug and tighten to 30Nm (21.5lb ft). Remove screws 5 and detach sump 3, then remove and discard gasket 2.

Refitting:

Thoroughly clean the inside of the sump and the joint faces on sump and crankcase. Using a new gasket, refit the sump with the fixing screws finger tight, then tighten the screws evenly and in a diagonal pattern to a final torque of 8Nm (6lb ft). Refill the engine with oil up to the MAX mark on the dipstick. Run the engine and check for oil leaks at the sump gasket.

1 : 8 Oil pump removal and servicing

Removal:

The oil pump can be removed with the engine in situ. Remove the sump. Remove the timing belt cover and align the pulley timing marks as described in **Section 1 : 3**. Select first or reverse gear and apply the handbrake fully to lock the engine against rotation, then slacken crankshaft pulley bolt 8 (see **FIG 1 : 24**). Make sure that the timing marks are still correctly aligned, then remove the timing belt as described in **Section 1 : 3**.

Unscrew and remove the crankshaft pulley bolt, then remove pulley 4 from the crankshaft, collecting the key (see **FIG 1 : 24**). Remove oil strainer 3 from crankcase and oil pump fixings. Remove the fixing screws and detach oil pump 5 from the crankcase. Discard the gasket.

Servicing:

Remove the fixing screws and detach pump rear cover 1, then remove pump gears 2. Remove seal 7 and pressure relief components 6 from the pump housing 5. Discard the oil seal.

Thoroughly clean all parts, including the oil strainer assembly, in a suitable solvent and allow them to dry. Examine the oil pump gears for wear, excessive backlash between teeth and for chipped or broken teeth. If any faults are found, the oil pump gears must be renewed as a matched pair. Examine the inner surface of pump rear

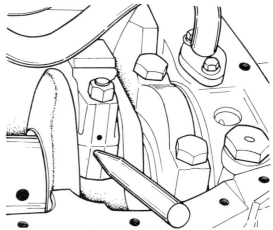

FIG 1 : 27   Marking connecting rods and caps for correct refitting

cover 1. Slight wear or scoring at this point can be remedied by surface grinding at a service station, but excessive wear or deep scoring will dictate renewal of the cover. Make a similar examination of the pump housing, which must be renewed if wear or damage is evident. Check the pressure relief valve for wear or damage and the valve spring for weakness or distortion. Renew parts as necessary.

Reassemble the pump in the reverse order of dismantling. Refit the pump assembly to the crankcase, using a new gasket, and tighten the fixing screws to 8Nm (6 lb ft). Install the oil strainer assembly, using a new gasket between flange and oil pump. Fit a new oil seal as described in **Section 1 : 11**, then refit the crankshaft pulley and install the pulley bolt finger tight. Refit the sump as described in **Section 1 : 7**.

Install the toothed timing belt as described in **Section 1 : 3**, then tighten the pulley fixing bolt to 80Nm (58lb ft) with the engine locked against rotation as described previously. Check for correct alignment of the timing marks and correct the tension of the toothed belt as described in **Section 1 : 3**, then fit the belt front cover

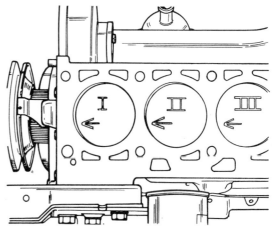

FIG 1 : 28   Marking pistons for correct refitting

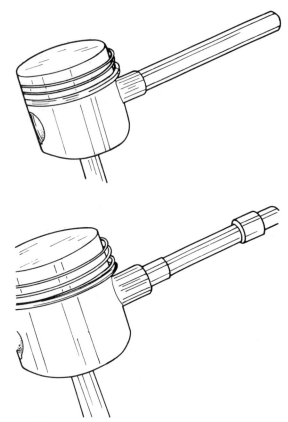

FIG 1:29   Gudgeon pin removal and installation

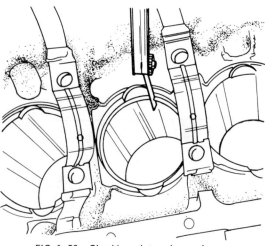

FIG 1:30   Checking piston ring end gap

1:9 External oil filter

The oil filter is of the renewable cartridge type and should be renewed at the intervals stated in the owners handbook. To do this, unscrew the oil filter cartridge as shown in **FIG 1:25** and discard it.

Clean the filter mounting face on the engine then lightly coat the new seal with engine oil. Make sure that the seal is correctly fitted, then screw the new filter into place until it just contacts its seating. From this point tighten by hand only, according to the directions printed on the filter body. Do not overtighten the filter or oil leaks may result. A strap type tool may be used to remove the filter unit if it is to stiff to unscrew by hand, but never use anything but hand pressure to tighten the unit. On completion, check the engine oil level, start the engine then check for oil leaks around the filter unit.

1:10 Pistons and connecting rods

Removal:

The pistons and connecting rods can be removed with engine in situ, after removing the cylinder head and sump, but if after dismantling it is found that attention to the crankshaft bearing surfaces or to the cylinder bores is required, engine removal will be necessary as described in **Section 1:2**.

Remove the cylinder head as described in **Section 1:4**, the sump as described in **Section 1:7** and the oil strainer assembly as described in **Section 1:8**. **FIG 1:26** shows piston and connecting rod components.

Mark each connecting rod and its corresponding cap on the same side as shown in **FIG 1:27**, so that the components can be refitted in their original positions. Unscrew the nuts and remove all connecting rod caps. Mark the pistons with their cylinder number and installation position as shown in **FIG 1:28**. Remove the pistons and connecting rods through the top of their bores. Collect the upper and lower big-end bearing shells, keeping them in the correct order for refitting in their original positions if they are not to be renewed. Discard the connecting rod bolts and nuts as these must be renewed on reassembly.

Pistons and rings:

Clean carbon deposits from the piston crowns, then gently ease the rings from their grooves and remove them over the top of the pistons. Clean carbon from the piston ring grooves, for which job a piece broken from an old piston ring and ground to a chisel point will prove an ideal tool. Inspect the pistons for score marks or any signs of seizure, which would dictate renewal. If the pistons are to be removed from the connecting rods, insert a thin bladed tool through the access groove in the bottom of the gudgeon pin bore and lever out the retaining circlips (see 6 in **FIG 1:26**). Gudgeon pins are removed and installed with tools 10-508 and VW222A as shown in **FIG 1:29**. If the gudgeon pin is difficult to remove or install, heat the piston and connecting rod assembly in an oven to approximately 60°C (140°F).

Fit the piston rings one at a time into the bore from which they were removed, pushing them into the bottom of the bore by approximately 15mm, using the associated piston to push them into place and ensure squareness. Measure the gaps between the ends of the ring while it is

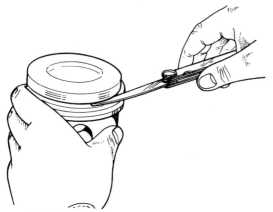

FIG 1:31 Checking piston ring side clearance

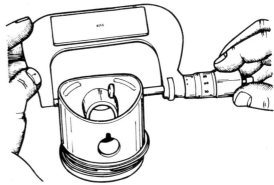

FIG 1:32 Measuring piston diameter

positioned in the bore, using feeler gauges as shown in **FIG 1:30**. This clearance should be between 0.30 and 0.45mm for top and centre rings and between 0.25 and 0.40mm for oil control ring, the wear limit being 1mm. Hold each ring in the piston groove from which it was removed as shown in **FIG 1:31**, then measure the side clearance with feeler gauges. Clearance should be 0.02 to 0.05mm for all rings, with a wear limit of 0.15mm. If the clearance measurements in either test are at or near the wear limits, new rings must be fitted. Excessive ring clearance can be responsible for high oil consumption and poor engine performance.

Check the cylinder bores for score marks and remove glaze and carbon deposits. Badly scored or worn surfaces will dictate a rebore to accept new pistons, this being a specialist job.

Check the clearance of each piston in its bore, measuring the outside diameter of the piston and the inside diameter of the bore and calculating the clearance. Pistons should be measured as shown in **FIG 1:32**, at a point approximately 16mm from the bottom edge and 90° to the gudgeon pin bore. Use an internal measuring gauge to check the diameter of cylinder bores, checking in two directions as shown at A and B in **FIG 1:33**, at a point 10mm below the top of the bore, at a point 10mm above the bottom of the bore and at the centre point.

Pistons and cylinder bores are arranged in honing groups, the particular honing group being marked next to the engine number on the crankcase. For honing group O, piston diameter is 69.48mm and cylinder bore diameter 69.51mm. For group I it is 69.49mm for pistons, 69.52mm for cylinders. For group II it is 69.50mm for pistons, 69.53mm for cylinder bores. In all cases, measured clearance between a new piston and bore is 0.02 to 0.04mm. The wear limit is 0.06mm. Excessive clearance will dictate the fitting of new pistons and, possibly, reboring of the cylinder bores. Reboring is a specialist job.

When refitting piston rings to the pistons, arrange them so that the ring gaps are spaced at 120° intervals around the piston circumference.

Connecting rods:

If there has been a big-end bearing failure, the crankpin must be examined for damage and for transfer of

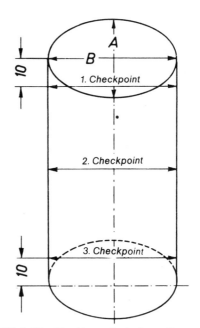

FIG 1:33 Checking cylinder bore diameter

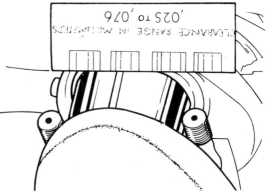

FIG 1:34 Checking connecting rod bearing clearance

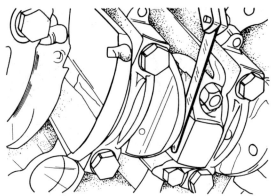

FIG 1:35   Checking connecting rod bearing side play

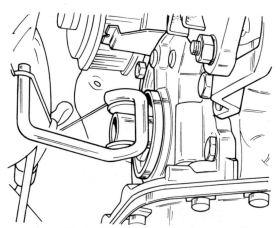

FIG 1:36   Pulley end crankshaft seal removal

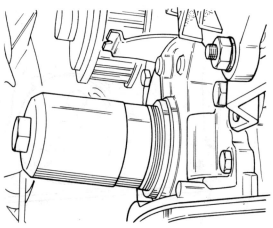

FIG 1:37   Pulley end crankshaft seal installation

metal to its surface. The oilway in the crankshaft must be checked to ensure that there is no obstruction. Big-end bearing clearance can be checked by the use of Plastigage, which is the trade name for a precisely calibrated plastic filament. The filament is laid along the bearing to be measured for working clearance, the bearing cap fitted and the bolts tightened to the specified torque. The bearing is then dismantled and the width of the flattened filament measured with the scale supplied with the material, as shown in **FIG 1:34**. The figure thus measured is the actual bearing clearance. Both main and big-end bearing clearances are measured in a similar manner.

Requirements for the use of Plastigage:

1 Each main bearing must be measured separately and none of the remaining bearing caps must be fitted during the operation.
2 The bearing surfaces must be clean and free from oil.
3 The crankshaft must not be turned during the measuring procedure.
4 The point at which the measurement is taken must be close to the respective dead centre position.
5 No hammer blows must be applied to the bearing or cap.

Procedure:

Place a length of plastic filament identical to the width of the bearing on the crankshaft journal, then fit the main or big-end bearing cap with liners and tighten to the specified torque. For big-end bearings this is 30Nm (21.5lb ft) plus a further 90° (quarter turn); for main bearings it is 65Nm (47lb ft).

Remove the bearing cap and measure the width of the flattened filament to obtain the running clearance for that bearing. For big-end bearings clearance should be 0.02 to 0.076mm with a wear limit of 0.095mm, for main bearings clearance should be 0.036 to 0.095mm with a wear limit of 0.105mm. If the bearing running clearance is too high, new bearing shells must be selected by the measurement procedure to bring the running clearance to within the specified limits.

While the connecting rod big-end bearing is assembled, check the side clearance as shown in **FIG 1:35**. This should be between 0.05 and 0.31mm with a wear limit of 0.4mm. When the crankshaft and all bearings are installed, check crankshaft end float at the centre main bearing position. This should be between 0.07 and 0.18mm with a wear limit of 0.2mm. Excessive big-end sideplay will dictate the fitting of a new connecting rod, excessive crankshaft end play will dictate the fitting of new flanged centre main bearing shells (see **Section 1:12**).

Refit the pistons and connecting rods in the reverse order of removal using a suitable piston ring clamp when entering the rings into the cylinder bores. Lubricate piston and big-end bearing surfaces with engine oil. Make sure that all components are refitted in their original positions. Note that the marks on the connecting rod bolt flanges must face the pulley end of the engine. Fit new connecting rod bolts and nuts and tighten to 30Nm (21.5lb ft) then tighten a further 90° (quarter turn). Always make sure that the connecting rod bearing shells are correctly fitted, with their tabs engaged in the slots in the connecting rod and bearing cap.

1:11 Crankshaft oil seals

The crankshaft oil seal at either side of the engine can be removed without the need for engine removal.

Pulley end seal:

Remove the toothed timing belt as described in **Section 1:3**, then remove the crankshaft pulley as described in **Section 1:8**. Refer to **FIG 1:36** and remove the old seal with tool 10-219. Use tool 10-203 as shown in **FIG 1:37** to install the new seal. Refit and tension the toothed timing belt as described in **Section 1:3**.

Flywheel end seal:

Refer to **Chapter 6** and remove the transmission. Remove the clutch assembly as described in **Chapter 5**. Lock the flywheel against rotation using tool 10-201 or similar as shown in **FIG 1:38**, then slacken the six flywheel retaining bolts. Support the weight of the flywheel, remove the retaining bolts then remove the flywheel from the end of the crankshaft.

Remove the flange then lever out the seal, using a screwdriver as shown in **FIG 1:39**. Use the sleeve part of tool 2003 to correctly align the new seal in the bore, then draw the seal in flush with the plate part of the same tool as shown in **FIG 1:40**.

Refit the components in the reverse order of removal, noting that the flywheel mounting bolts must be degreased and coated with sealant D6 or suitable substitute before installation. Tighten the flywheel mounting bolts alternately and evenly to 75Nm (54lb ft).

1:12 Crankshaft and main bearings

In order to remove the crankshaft the engine and transmission must first be removed as described in **Section 1:2**, then the transmission removed as described in **Chapter 6** and the clutch removed as described in **Chapter 5**. Remove the oil pump and strainer assembly as described in **Section 1:8** and the flywheel as described in **Section 1:11**.

Refer to **FIG 1:41**. Remove end plate 10 with gasket 9. Note that the main bearing caps are marked 1 to 5 from the pulley end of the engine to ensure refitting in their original locations. Remove the bolts and detach the bearing caps and lower bearing shell halves. Carefully lift out the crankshaft then remove the upper bearing shell halves from the crankcase. Keep all bearing shells in the correct order for refitting in their original positions if they are not to be renewed.

If there has been a main bearing failure, the crankshaft journal must be checked for damage and for transfer of metal to its surface. The oilways in the crankshaft must be checked to ensure that there is no obstruction. Main bearing clearance can be checked by the use of Plastigage, in the manner described in **Section 1:10** for big-end bearings the procedure being the same. If there is any doubt about the condition of the crankshaft it should be taken to a specialist for more detailed checks.

Examine the starter ring gear on the flywheel. If the teeth are broken or worn, a new unit should be fitted. When reassembling the crankshaft to the crankcase, check the end float as described in **Section 1:10**.

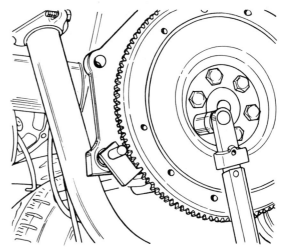

FIG 1:38   Flywheel removal

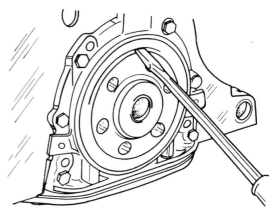

FIG 1:39   Flywheel end seal removal

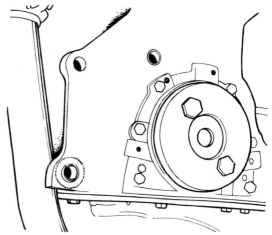

FIG 1:40   Flywheel end seal installation

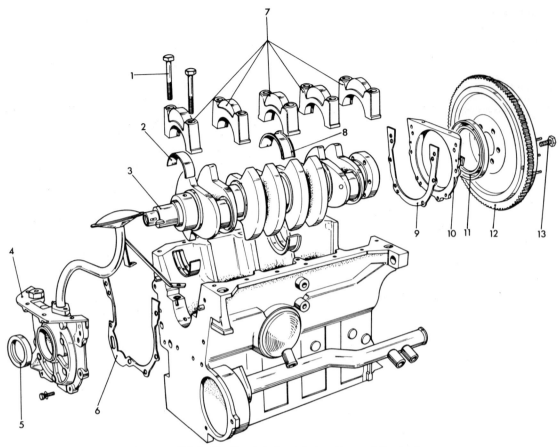

FIG 1 : 41   Crankshaft, main bearings and flywheel

Key to Fig 1 : 41   1 Cap bolt   2 Plain bearing shell   3 Crankshaft   4 Oil pump   5 Seal   6 Gasket   7 Bearing caps
8 Flanged bearing shell   9 Gasket   10 End plate   11 Seal   12 Flywheel   13 Flywheel bolt

Refit the crankshaft in the reverse order of removal, making sure that the bearing shells and main bearing caps are refitted in their original positions. Use new gaskets and seals throughout. Note that the upper bearing shells fitted to the crankcase are all provided with lubricating grooves. No lubricating grooves are provided in the lower bearing shells which are fitted to the caps. Both upper and lower shells for the centre main bearing (No. 3) are provided with flanged edges to control crankshaft end float. Lubricate the bearing shells before installing the crankshaft. Fit the bearing caps in the correct order and tighten the bolts to 65Nm (47lb ft). Refit the remaining components in the reverse order of removal, then refit the engine to the car as described in **Section 1 : 2.**

1 : 13 Fault diagnosis

(a) Engine will not start

1 Defective coil
2 Faulty distributor capacitor
3 Dirty, pitted or incorrectly set contact points
4 Ignition wires loose or insulation faulty
5 Water on spark plug leads
6 Battery discharged, corrosion of terminals
7 Faulty or jammed starter
8 Sparking plug leads wrongly connected
9 Vapour lock in fuel pipes
10 Defective fuel pump
11 Overchoking or underchoking
12 Blocked fuel filter or carburetter jet
13 Leaking valves
14 Sticking valves
15 Valve timing incorrect
16 Ignition timing incorrect

(b) Engine stalls

1 Check 1, 2, 3, 4, 5, 10, 11, 12, 13 and 14 in (a)
2 Sparking plugs defective or gaps incorrect
3 Retarded ignition
4 Mixture too weak
5 Water in fuel system
6 Petrol tank vent blocked
7 Incorrect valve clearances

(c) Engine idles badly

1 Check 2 and 7 in (b)
2 Air leak at manifold joints
3 Carburetter adjustment wrong
4 Air leak in carburetter
5 Over rich mixture
6 Worn piston rings
7 Worn valve stems or guides
8 Weak exhaust valve springs

(d) Engine misfires

1 Check 1, 2, 3, 4, 5, 8, 10, 12, 13, 14, 15 and 16 in (a)
2 Weak or broken valve springs

(e) Engine overheats (see Chapter 4)

(f) Compression low

1 Check 13 and 14 in (a); 6 and 7 in (c); and 2 in (d)
2 Worn piston ring grooves
3 Scored or worn cylinder bores

(g) Engine lacks power

1 Check 3, 10, 11, 12, 13, 14, 15 and 16 in (a); 2, 3, 4 and 7 in (b); 6 and 7 in (c); and 2 in (d). Also check (e) and (f)
2 Leaking gaskets or seals
3 Fouled sparking plugs
4 Automatic advance not working

(h) Burnt valves or seats

1 Check 13 and 14 in (a); 7 in (b); and 2 in (d). Also check (e)
2 Excessive carbon round valve seats and head

(j) Sticking valves

1 Check 2 in (d)
2 Bent valve stem
3 Scored valve stem or guide
4 Incorrect valve clearances

(k) Excessive cylinder wear

1 Check 11 in (a)
2 Lack of oil
3 Dirty oil
4 Piston rings gummed up or broken
5 Badly fitting piston rings
6 Connecting rod bent

(l) Excessive oil consumption

1 Check 6 and 7 in (c); and check (k)
2 Ring gaps too wide
3 Oil return holes in piston choked with carbon
4 Scored cylinders
5 Oil level too high
6 External oil leaks

(m) Crankshaft and connecting rod bearing failure

1 Check 2 and 6 in (k)
2 Restricted oilways
3 Worn journals or crankpins
4 Loose bearing caps
5 Extremely low oil pressure

(n) Engine vibration

1 Loose alternator bolts
2 Engine mountings loose or defective
3 Misfiring due to mixture, ignition or mechanical faults

NOTES

CHAPTER 2

THE FUEL SYSTEM

2:1 Description

Fuel from the rear mounted tank is supplied to the carburetter by a mechanical type fuel pump operated from a special eccentric on the engine camshaft. The pump is mounted on the side of the cylinder head.

A Solex 31 PICT-5 carburetter is fitted, this unit being specially designed to provide a balanced and compensated fuel/air mixture for minimum toxic exhaust emissions. An automatic or manual choke may be fitted depending on model type.

Paper cartridge type air cleaner units are used, fitted to the carburetter intake.

2:2 Air cleaner

The air cleaner element should be renewed at the intervals recommended in the service booklet. To remove the element, release the spring clips and detach the air cleaner top cover (see **FIG 2:1**). If the element is to be renewed, remove the old element and discard it. Wipe the inside of the air cleaner body and cover to remove dirt and grease, then fit the new element, replace the cover and secure with the spring clips.

To remove the air cleaner body, unscrew the fixings securing it in position. Disconnect the pipes from their fittings on the air cleaner assembly, then remove the assembly complete. Refitting is a reversal of the removal procedure.

2:3 Fuel pump

Testing:

Before testing the pump, ensure that the fuel tank vent system is not blocked. If a vent system blockage is suspected, remove the fuel filler cap and clean the vent hose **A** with compressed air (see **FIG 2:2**). This done, check that air can pass freely through connecting tube **B**. If air flows freely through tube **B**, the fuel tank vent is functioning correctly (see **FIG 2:3**).

If the vent system is clear and it is still suspected that fuel is not reaching the carburetter, disconnect the carburetter feed pipe and hold a suitable container under the end of the pipe. Turn the engine over a few times with the starter and watch for fuel squirting from the end of the pipe, which indicates that the pump is working.

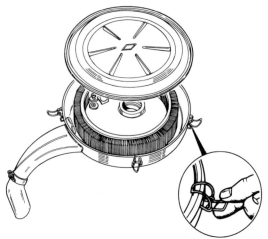

FIG 2:1   Air filter element removal

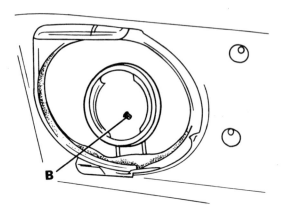

FIG 2:3   Checking vent air passage

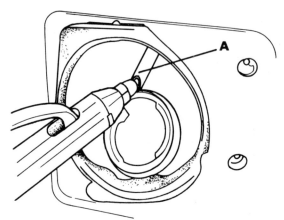

FIG 2:2   Clearing tank vent system

If so, check the float needle in the carburetter for possible sticking.

Reduced fuel flow can be caused by blocked fuel pipes or a clogged filter. Check the filter element in the fuel pump. To do this, remove the single screw and detach the pump cover (see **FIG 2:4**). Carefully remove the filter and wash it in clean petrol, using a small brush to remove stubborn deposits. If the filter is damaged or will not clean up properly it should be renewed. Remove any sediment from the filter housing, then refit the cover and tighten the screw.

If an obstructed pipeline appears to be the cause of the trouble, it may be cleared with compressed air. Disconnect the pipeline at the pump and carburetter. **Do not pass compressed air through the pump or the valves will be damaged.** If there is an obstruction between the pump and the tank, remove the tank filler cap before blowing the pipe through from the pump end.

If the pump delivers insufficient fuel, suspect an air leak between the pump and the tank, dirt under the pump valves or faulty valve seatings. If no fuel is delivered, suspect a sticking valve or a faulty pump diaphragm.

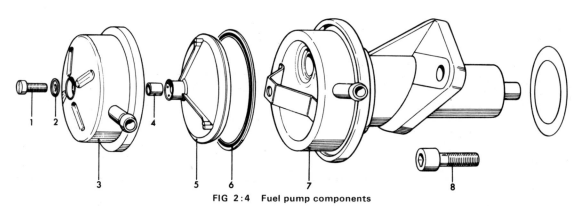

FIG 2:4   Fuel pump components

Key to Fig 2:4   1 Screw   2 Sealing washer   3 Cover   4 Spacer   5 Filter   6 Sealing ring   7 Pump body   8 Securing bolt

Test the action of the pump valves by blowing and sucking at the inlet and outlet points. Do this with the pump in situ, using a suitable piece of pipe connected to the pump inlet and outlet in turn. It should be possible to blow in through the pump inlet but not to suck air out, and it should be possible to suck air out of the pump outlet but not to blow air in. If the valves do not work properly according to this test, or if the pump is defective in any other way, a new unit must be fitted as the pump is serviced only as a complete assembly.

Removal:

Disconnect the fuel pipes from the fuel pump and fit plugs to the pipes to prevent fuel leaks before removing the pump from the engine. Remove the two fixing bolts and detach the fuel pump (see **FIG 2:4**). Remove the spacer and gasket.

Refitting:

This is a reversal of the removal procedure. Always use a new gasket. Tighten the fixing bolts evenly to avoid distortion of the mounting flange.

2:4 Carburetter adjustments

If engine idling speed is incorrect, or if the idle is rough or unreliable, the problem can usually be cured by carrying out the accelerator and choke cable adjustments and the slow running adjustments described in this section. However, if this does not set the idling speed correctly, or if the carburetter has been overhauled, the adjustment procedures described in **Section 2:5** should be carried out, followed by the adjustment procedures given in this section.

Accelerator cable adjustment:

Slacken the clamp securing the accelerator cable to the lever on the carburetter. Have an assistant press the accelerator pedal fully to the floor. Move the throttle lever on the carburetter to the full throttle position, then tighten the clamp screw. Release the accelerator pedal and check the engine idle is satisfactory.

Cable choke adjustment:

Slacken the locking screw securing the choke cable to the operating lever on the carburetter. Push in the choke control beside the steering column inside the car fully, then pull it out by approximately 3 to 5mm. With the cable in this position, hold the choke fully open with the lever on the carburetter while firmly tightening the cable locking screw. The cable will then be set with the correct amount of free play. Check for smooth operation through the full range of choke control movement.

Slow-running adjustment:

Note that idle speed adjustments will only be effective if the sparking plugs, contact points and ignition system are in good order. The engine must be at normal operating temperature before starting the adjustment procedure.

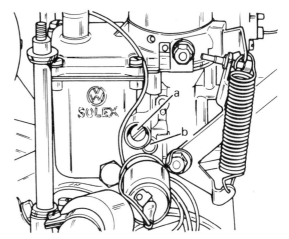

FIG 2:5 Idle air control screw a and idle mixture control screw b

Tachometer equipment will be needed to accurately set the idle speed. On completion, the CO (carbon monoxide) content of the exhaust gas should be checked, and further fine adjustments made to bring the level to within prescribed limits in areas where legal controls are applicable. If suitable analytical equipment is not available for this purpose, the CO content should be checked by a service station.

Run the engine until it reaches normal operating temperature and check that the choke is completely open. Refer to **FIG 2:5**, which shows the idle air control screw **a** and the idle mixture control screw **b**. Allow the engine to idle, with the gearlever in neutral and the handbrake applied. Screws **a** and **b** must be adjusted a little at a time and alternately, until a smooth idle at 950 ± 50rev/min is achieved. Note that the idle mixture system and the idle air system are directly related to each other, so adjustments must be made by turning the two screws alternately.

The CO content of the exhaust gas should be between 2 and 3 per cent by volume. If the higher figure is exceeded, further adjustments to the idle setting screws must be carried out to bring the figure to within limits. If CO content is below 2 per cent, it is not recommended to increase this volume unless the engine runs roughly or stalls due to an excessively lean fuel/air mixture.

2:5 Carburetter servicing

Removal:

Remove the air cleaner assembly as described in **Section 2:2**. Disconnect the accelerator and choke cables from the levers on the carburetter. Disconnect the vacuum advance pipe that leads to the distributor. Disconnect the fuel feed pipe, plugging the end of the pipe to prevent loss of fuel and entry of dirt. Detach the electrical connector from the carburetter, if fitted. Unscrew the two nuts from the mounting studs and lift the carburetter from the inlet manifold flange, collecting the flange gasket.

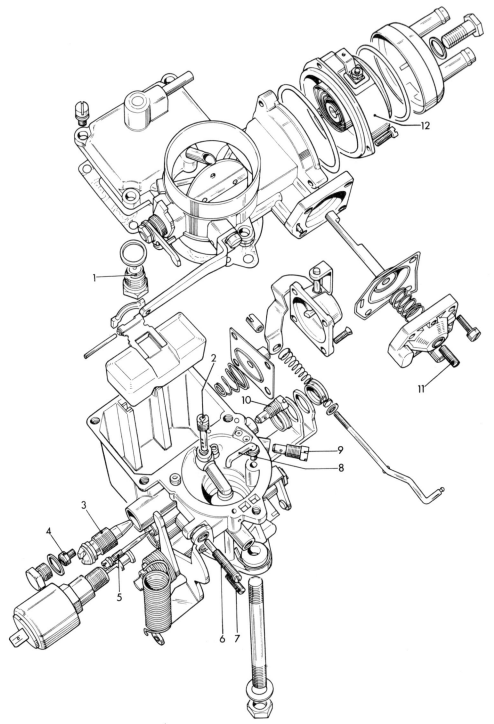

FIG 2:6 Carburetter components

Key to Fig 2:6   1 Needle valve   2 Air correction jet   3 Idle air control screw   4 Main jet   5 Idle mixture control screw
6 Throttle cold start adjustment   7 Throttle basic adjustment   8 Accelerator pump injection tube   9 Idle jet   10 Plug
11 Choke gap adjuster   12 Automatic choke

Refitting:

This is a reversal of the removal procedure, using a new flange gasket. On completion, carry out the accelerator and choke cable adjustments and, if necessary, the slow-running adjustment procedure, as described in **Section 2:4**.

Dismantling:

Refer to **FIG 2:6**. Disconnect the external linkages from the carburetter control levers. Remove the fixing screws and lift off the carburetter top cover. Discard the cover gasket. Unscrew the needle valve assembly from the top cover, collecting the sealing washer. Do not remove the choke plate or shaft unless the components are to be renewed.

Release the hinge pin and lift the float assembly from the float chamber. Remove the idle air control screw and the idle mixture control screw, counting the number of turns taken to remove each screw so that they can be refitted in their original positions to provide a basic idle setting. Remove the jets from the carburetter body, noting their positions for correct refitting. Remove the screws and detach the accelerator pump cover, then remove the diaphragm and spring.

Do not remove the throttle plate or shaft unless they are to be renewed.

If shafts, levers and plate valves are to be dismantled, mark the components so that they will be reassembled in their correct relative positions.

Servicing:

Clean all parts in petrol or an approved carburetter cleaner, then examine them for wear or damage. Renew any faulty parts. Clean jets and passages thoroughly, using compressed air, clean petrol and a small stiff brush. An old toothbrush will be found ideal for this purpose.

Do not use cloth for cleaning purposes, as small fibres may remain after cleaning and clog the jets or passages. Never use a wire probe as this will damage or enlarge the jets.

If a jet has a blockage which cannot be cleared with compressed air, use a single bristle from a stiff brush for the purpose. If this method is unsuccessful, renew the jet. Details of jet and carburetter specifications are given in **Technical Data** in the **Appendix**. Note that a plug is fitted to the carburetter idling system in place of the usual auxiliary fuel jet (see **FIG 2:7**). **This plug looks like a proper auxiliary fuel jet but must never be replaced by a drilled fuel jet.**

Make sure that all sediment is cleaned from the float chamber and check the float for damage or leakage. Float leakage can generally be detected by shaking float and listening for the sound of fuel splash inside. Renew the float if any fault is found.

Check the float needle valve assembly carefully, renewing the assembly if there is any sign of a ridge on the tapered valve seat. A damaged needle valve can lead to flooding by failing to cut off the fuel supply properly when the float chamber is full, or may stick in the closed position and prevent sufficient fuel from reaching the float chamber.

Examine the tips of the idle control screws and renew them if there is any sign of wear or damage. Check the

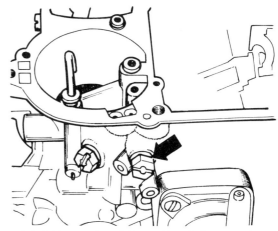

FIG 2:7 Location of the auxiliary fuel system plug

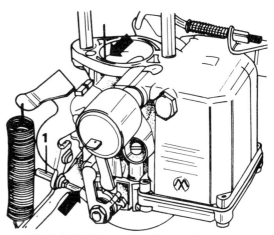

FIG 2:8 Cold start throttle gap adjustment

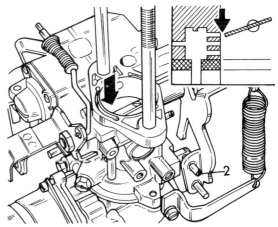

FIG 2:9 Basic throttle gap adjustment

FIG 2:10 Adjusting automatic choke

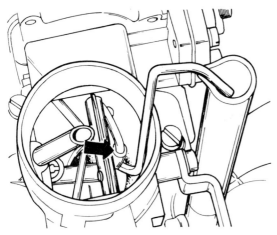

FIG 2:11 Checking accelerator pump injection rate

accelerator pump diaphragm for splits, tears, deformities and for hardening of the material. Renew the diaphragm if not in perfect condition.

Reassembly:

Reassemble the carburetter in the reverse order of dismantling, using new gaskets and seals throughout. Take care not to overtighten the jets or component fixing screws to avoid stripping the threads in the light alloy castings. Make sure that the sealing washer is correctly fitted beneath the needle valve assembly. A washer of the correct thickness must always be installed as this controls the float level.

Carry out the component adjustments described next. These done and the carburetter fully assembled, refit to the car and connect the hoses and linkages, making sure that the linkages operate smoothly and open the throttle and choke fully. Finally, carry out the adjustment procedures described in **Section 2:4**.

Throttle gap adjustment:

Cold start setting:

Refer to **FIG 2:8**. Close the choke completely by setting the adjusting screw 1 on the highest step of the stepped disc. Hold a bar or drill of appropriate diameter (see **Technical Data**) in the carburetter bore as shown by the upper arrow, then turn adjusting screw 1 until it is just touched by the throttle valve.

Basic throttle gap adjustment:

Make sure that the choke is open completely, then turn adjusting screw 2 until the throttle plate justs barely covers the lower bypass bore (see **FIG 2:9**).

Checking and adjusting automatic choke (where fitted):

Unscrew choke cover holder and remove the cover with intermediate ring. Refer to **FIG 2:10**. Press pulldown linkage against stop with a screwdriver. Press choke towards 'close' until the operating lever rests against stop of linkage. Check that the choke gap is 5.0 ± 0.15mm with a drill bit of corresponding diameter and adjust with the screw 3 if necessary.

Fuel level adjustment:

The fuel level in the carburetter float chamber is controlled by the float and needle valve positions. The needle valve assembly should always be fitted with a sealing washer of 2mm thickness (standard). With the correct sealing washer fitted and a float assembly in good condition, it is unlikely that the fuel level will be incorrect. However, if an incorrect fuel level is suspected, a check should be made with the carburetter installed. Run the engine at idle for a few moments to stabilise the fuel level, then switch off. Make sure that the car is standing on level ground. Remove the carburetter float chamber carefully to avoid damaging the gasket. Use a suitable ruler to measure the distance between the fuel in the carburetter float chamber and the top face of the float chamber. This dimension should be 21 ± 1mm. If the level is incorrect, check that the sealing washer beneath

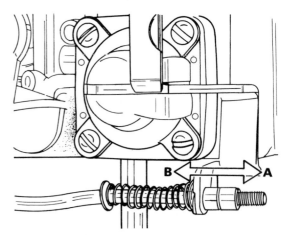

FIG 2:12 Accelerator pump adjustment

the needle valve assembly is of the correct thickness and that the float assembly is not damaged or distorted. Renew any faulty parts. If all components are in good condition, the fuel level can be corrected by changing the thickness of washer beneath the needle valve assembly. This procedure will have to be carried out on a trial and error basis, until the correct setting is achieved.

Accelerator pump injection rate adjustment:

When the carburetter is assembled and fitted to the car, test the fuel injection rate. To do this, connect a suitable piece of tubing, such as tool VW-119, to the accelerator pump injector nozzle and lead the free end into a measuring cylinder. Move the throttle lever to and fro quickly over 10 full strokes. The correct quantity of fuel injected for a single stroke is 0.75 to 1.05cc (see **FIG 2:11**). The quantity stated, multiplied by 10, should equal the quantity collected in the measuring glass. Measuring the quantity delivered from 10 strokes gives a more accurate indication than attempting to measure a single stroke only. If the injection rate is incorrect, refer to **FIG 2:12** and turn the nut on the operating rod to alter the amount of fuel delivered. Adjust towards **A** to increase, towards **B** to decrease. If the correct injection rate cannot be achieved by this means, check the accelerator pump diaphragm as described previously. If a blockage in the accelerator pump nozzle is suspected, clear the nozzle with compressed air. Make sure that the accelerator pump nozzle is adjusted so that the fuel from the nozzle enters the carburetter through the throttle gap.

2:6 Fault diagnosis

(a) Leakage or insufficient fuel delivered

1 Air vent to tank obstructed
2 Fuel pipes blocked
3 Air leaks at pipe connections
4 Fuel filter blocked
5 Pump gaskets faulty
6 Pump diaphragm defective
7 Pump valves sticking or seating badly

(b) Excessive fuel consumption

1 Carburetter requires adjustment
2 Fuel leakage
3 Sticking choke control
4 Dirty air cleaner
5 Worn jets in carburetter
6 Excessive engine temperature
7 Idling speed too high

(c) Idling speed too high

1 Rich fuel mixture
2 Throttle control sticking
3 Choke control sticking
4 Worn throttle valve

(d) Noisy fuel pump

1 Loose pump mountings
2 Air leaks on suction side of diaphragm
3 Obstruction in fuel pipeline
4 Clogged fuel filter

(e) No fuel delivery

1 Float needle valve stuck
2 Tank vent system blocked
3 Defective pump diaphragm
4 Pump valve stuck
5 Pipeline obstructed
6 Bad air leak on suction side of pump

NOTES

CHAPTER 3

THE IGNITION SYSTEM

3:1 Description

The ignition system is conventional, comprising an ignition coil, distributor and contact breaker assembly. The distributor incorporates automatic timing control by centrifugal mechanism and a vacuum operated unit. As engine speed increases, the centrifugal action of rotating weights pivoting against the tension of small springs moves the contact breaker cam relative to the distributor drive shaft and progressively advances the ignition. The vacuum control unit is connected by small bore pipe to a fitting on the carburetter. At high degrees of vacuum the unit advances the ignition, but under load, at reduced vacuum, the unit progressively retards the ignition.

The ignition coil is wound as an auto-transformer with the primary and secondary windings connected in series, the common junction being connected to the contact breaker with the positive feed from the battery going to the opposite terminal of the LT windings via the ignition switch. On earlier models the LT current is supplied to the coil through a resistor which reduces nominal battery voltage to approximately 9 volts at the coil terminal. This resistor is bypassed when the starter is in operation, so that full battery voltage is supplied to the coil. The coil then provides increased voltage to the HT

system for maximum sparking plug efficiency when the engine is being started.

When the contact breaker points are closed, current flows in the coil primary winding, magnetising the core and setting up a fairly strong magnetic field. Each time the contacts open, the battery current is cut off and the magnetic field collapses, inducing a high current in the primary winding and a high voltage in the secondary. The primary current is used to charge the capacitor connected across the contacts and the flow is high and virtually instantaneous. It is this high current peak which induces the surge in the secondary winding to produce the sparking voltage across the plug points. Without the capacitor the current peak would be much smaller and the sparking voltage considerably reduced, in fact to a point where it would be insufficient to fire the mixture in the engine cylinders. The capacitor, therefore, serves the dual purpose of minimising contact breaker wear and providing the necessary high charging surge to ensure a powerful spark.

3:2 Routine maintenance

Pull off the two spring clips and remove the distributor cap. Pull off the rotor arm and remove the dust cover to gain access to the contact breaker points. **FIG 3:1** shows the contact breaker mechanism.

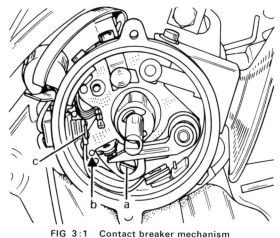

FIG 3:1   Contact breaker mechanism

Key to Fig 3:1   a Securing screw   **b** Adjustment point
c Connector

Lubrication:

Wipe clean the cam which opens the contact points and apply a thin smear of grease to the cam. If necessary, remove the bearing plate from the top of the distributor to improve access.

Adjusting the contact breaker points:

The most accurate method of setting the points gap is by using a dwell angle meter. With the connections made according to the instructions supplied with the particular meter being used, the dwell angle when the engine is cranked with the starter motor should be $47° \pm 3°$. Adjust the gap if necessary to achieve this figure.

If a dwell angle meter is not available the gap must be set by measurement with feeler gauges.

Turn the engine until one of the cams has opened the contact breaker points to their fullest extent, then check the gap between the points with clean feeler gauges. The correct gap is 0.4mm (0.016in). To adjust the gap, loosen screw **a** (**FIG 3:1**) and insert the blade of a screwdriver between adjusting pips **b**. Turn the screwdriver to open or close the points gap as necessary, then tighten screw **a** and recheck the gap. The distributor top bearing must always be in position when checking the points gap.

Cleaning the contact breaker points:

Use a fine carbordundum stone or special contact point file to polish the points if they are dirty or pitted, taking care to keep the faces flat and square. If the points are too worn to clean up in this manner, they should be renewed. On completion, wipe away all dust with a cloth moistened in petrol then set the points gap as described previously.

Renewing the contact breaker points:

Remove screw **a** and pull off connector **c**. Lift out the contact points set. Wash the mating faces of the new contact points with methylated spirits to remove the protective coating. Fit the contact points set to the base plate and secure with the single screw. Push the connector on to the terminal. Set the contact points to the correct gap as described previously.

Checking rotor arm:

To check rotor arm insulation, fit the rotor in position and remove the central HT lead from the distributor cap. Hold the end of the lead approximately 12.0mm (0.5in) from the rotor centre contact. To avoid shocks, hold the lead well away from the end. With the ignition switched on, flick open the contact points. If a spark jumps the gap the rotor is faulty and must be renewed.

3:3 Ignition faults

If the engine runs unevenly, set it to idle at about 1000rev/min and, taking care not to touch any conducting part of the sparking plug leads, remove and replace each lead from its plug in turn. To avoid shocks during this operation it is best to wear a pair of thick gloves or to use insulated pliers. Doing this to a plug which is firing correctly will accentuate the uneven running but will make no difference if the plug is not firing.

Having by this means located the faulty cylinder, stop the engine and remove the plug lead. Pull back the insulation or remove the connector so that the end of the lead is exposed. Alternatively, use an extension piece, such as a small bar or drill, pushed into the plug connector. Hold the lead carefully to avoid shocks, so that the end is about 3mm ($\frac{1}{8}$in) away from the cylinder head. Crank the engine with the starter or flick open the contact points with the ignition switched on. A strong, regular spark confirms that the fault lies with the sparking plug which should be removed and cleaned as described in **Section 3:6**, or renewed if defective.

If the spark is weak and irregular, check the condition of the lead and, if it is perished or cracked, renew it and repeat the test. If no improvement results, check that the inside of the distributor cap is clean and dry and that there is no sign of tracking, which can be seen as a thin black line between the electrodes or to some metal part in contact with the cap. Tracking can only be cured by fitting a new cap. Check the carbon brush inside the cap for wear or damage, and check that it moves in and out freely against the pressure of its internal spring (see **FIG 3:2**). Check the brass segments in the cap for wear or burning. Renew the cap if any fault is found.

If these checks do not cure a weak HT spark, or if no spark can be obtained at the plug or lead, check the LT circuit as described next.

Testing the low tension circuit:

A test lamp can be used to check circuit continuity, but accurate checking of the components requires the use of a voltmeter due to the differing voltages supplied to the coil during starting and running.

Checking coil current supply:

Connect the voltmeter positive to the coil positive terminal and the voltmeter negative to a good earth on the car engine or body, then connect a jumper lead from the coil negative to a good earth.

To check the starting supply to the coil, turn the ignition key to the start position and crank the engine. While the engine is turning on the starter, the voltmeter should register at least 8 volts. A low or zero reading may be due to faulty contacts in the starter solenoid switch or to defective wiring. To check the running supply to the coil through the resistor, switch on the ignition without starting the engine, when the voltmeter should register 4.5 to 6.0 volts. A voltmeter reading outside the limits stated indicates a fault in the resistor.

Primary winding, contact breaker and capacitor check:

This check involves turning the engine, which should be carried out using a spanner of the correct size on the crankshaft pulley mounting bolt. Alternatively, select top gear, release the handbrake and push the car forwards to turn the engine. Apply the handbrake when the correct settings are obtained. In either case, the engine will be easier to turn if all of the sparking plugs are removed first. Connect the voltmeter positive to the coil negative terminal, and the voltmeter negative to a good earth on the engine or body.

Remove the distributor cap and position it to one side. Turn the engine until the contact points are open, then switch on the ignition. The voltmeter should register battery voltage (11.5 to 12.0 volts). If there is no reading, there is a break in the coil primary winding or there is a shortcircuit in either the contact breaker connection or in the capacitor.

Turn the engine until the contact breaker points are closed, then switch on the ignition. The voltmeter reading should be zero to 0.2 volt. If over 0.2 volt, the contact points are dirty, the contact breaker plate and/or distributor housing earth is faulty, or the wire between coil and distributor has a break in it.

If the contact breaker points are blackened and there is a lot of arcing at the points when they are flicked open, suspect a faulty capacitor. The best method of testing a capacitor is by substitution. Disconnect the original capacitor and connect a new one of the right type between the low tension terminal on the distributor and earth for test purposes. The capacitor is shown at 6 in **FIG 3:2**. If a new capacitor is proved to be required, it can then be properly fitted.

3:4 Distributor, removal and refitting

Removal:

FIG 3:2 shows the distributor components. Remove the distributor cap and place it to one side, then disconnect the thin wire fitted between the terminal on the side of the distributor and the coil. Pull off the pipe connected to vacuum unit 8.

Turn the engine until the distributor rotor arm is pointing towards the mark on the distributor body as shown in **FIG 3:3**, and the mark on the crankshaft pulley is aligned with the second pointer on the front of the engine as shown in **FIG 3:4**. The marks will align correctly every second revolution of the engine. The procedure aligns the engine to the firing point for No. 1 cylinder and this will facilitate correct refitting of the distributor provided that the engine is not turned while the distributor is removed.

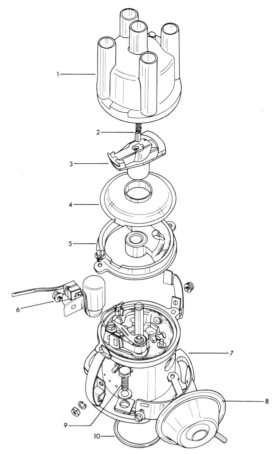

FIG 3:2   Distributor components

Key to Fig 3:2   1 Distributor cap   2 Carbon brush
3 Rotor arm   4 Dust cover   5 Top bearing plate
6 Capacitor   7 Distributor body   8 Vacuum unit
9 Distributor mounting bolt   10 Sealing ring

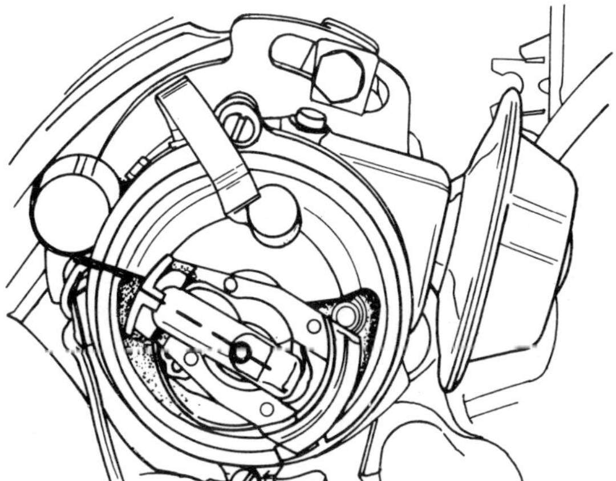

FIG 3:3   Aligning distributor rotor with TDC mark

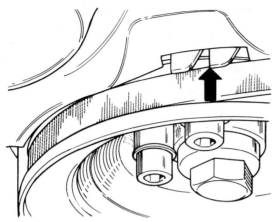

FIG 3:4 Aligning crankshaft pulley mark with TDC pointer

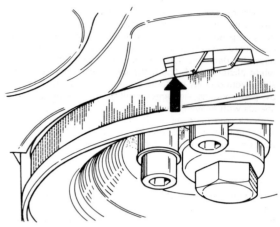

FIG 3:5 Aligning pulley mark with first pointer to set ignition timing to 10° BTDC

Remove the two fixing bolts shown at 9 in **FIG 3:2**, then remove the distributor from the cylinder head. Remove sealing ring 10.

Refitting:

Check the distributor sealing ring and renew it if not in perfect condition. If the engine has not been turned while the distributor was removed, align the distributor rotor as shown in **FIG 3:3** and fit the distributor to the cylinder head. Turn the rotor a little as necessary until the distributor shaft engages with the drive. Turn the distributor body a little if necessary to realign the rotor and mark, then fit the distributor attachment bolts finger tight. Carry out the ignition timing procedure as described in **Section 3:5**.

If the engine has been turned and the timing setting lost, the engine must be reset at the firing point for No. 1 cylinder. To do this, either remove the camshaft cover and turn the engine until the cams for No. 1 (righthand) cylinder are clear of the rockers, or remove the sparking plug from No. 1 cylinder and turn the engine until compression can be felt by a thumb placed over the plug hole. From this position, turn the engine a little more as necessary to align the pulley timing mark with the second pointer as shown in **FIG 3:4**. Install the distributor as described previously then check the timing as described in **Section 3:5**.

3:5 Timing the ignition

Remove the distributor cap and place it to one side. Turn the engine in the normal direction of forward rotation until the timing mark on the crankshaft pulley aligns with the first pointer on the front of the engine as shown in **FIG 3:5**, and the distributor rotor arm is pointing towards the mark on the distributor housing as shown in **FIG 3:3**. The marks will correctly align once in every two engine revolutions. Slacken the distributor mounting bolts as shown at 9 in **FIG 3:2** so that the distributor housing can just be turned by hand.

Connect a 12-volt test lamp in parallel with the contact breaker points. One lead will go to the terminal on the side of the distributor and one to earth. Turn the distributor body anticlockwise as far as possible to ensure that the contact points are fully closed. Now switch on the ignition and turn the distributor body very slowly in a clockwise direction until the lamp just lights. Without moving the distributor from this position, tighten the distributor mounting screws. The correct torque for these screws 10.0Nm (7.2lb ft). Refit the distributor cap.

Stroboscopic timing:

If this method of timing is used, the vacuum pipe must be removed from the distributor and the end of the pipe plugged with a suitable bolt or sealed by clamping. Slacken the distributor mounting bolts and connect the stroboscopic equipment according to the manufacturer's instructions. Engine idling speed must be adjusted to 950 ± 50rev/min or the centrifugal advance mechanism will operate and give a false reading. Turn the distributor body as necessary to align the pulley timing mark with the first pointer on the engine as shown in **FIG 3:5**, then tighten the distributor mounting bolts. Recheck the setting before disconnecting the stroboscopic equipment.

3:6 Sparking plugs

Inspect and clean sparking plugs regularly. When removing sparking plugs, ensure that their recesses are clean and dry so that nothing can fall into the cylinders. Have sparking plugs cleaned on an abrasive blasting machine and tested under pressure with the electrode gaps correctly set at 0.7mm (0.027in). The electrodes should be filed until they are bright and parallel. The gaps must always be set by adjusting the earth electrode. Never attempt to bend the centre electrode. As a general rule, plugs should be cleaned and tested at about 6000 mile intervals and renewed at about 12,000 mile intervals or before if badly worn.

Inspection of the deposits on the electrodes can be helpful when tuning. Normally, from mixed periods of high and low speed driving, the deposits should be powdery and range in colour from brown to greyish-tan. There will also be slight wear of the electrodes. Long periods of constant speed driving or low speed city driving will give white or yellowish deposits. Dry, black fluffy deposits are due to incomplete combustion and indicate running with a rich mixture, excessive idling and, possibly, defective ignition. Overheated plugs have a white blistered look about the centre electrode and the side electrode may be badly eroded. This may be caused by poor cooling, incorrect ignition or sustained high speeds with heavy loads.

Black, wet deposits result from oil in the combustion chamber from worn pistons, rings, valve stems or guides. Sparking plugs which run hotter may alleviate the problem but the cure is an engine overhaul.

Sparking plug leads:

Renew high tension leads if they are defective in any way. Inspect for broken, swollen or deteriorated insulation which can be the cause of current leakage, especially in wet weather conditions. Also check the condition of the plug connectors at the ends of the leads.

3:7 Fault diagnosis

(a) Engine will not fire

1 Battery discharged
2 Contact breaker points dirty, pitted or maladjusted
3 Distributor cap dirty, cracked or tracking
4 Carbon brush worn or stuck in mounting
5 Faulty cable or loose connection in low tension circuit
6 Distributor rotor arm cracked
7 Faulty coil
8 Broken contact breaker spring
9 Contact points stuck open

(b) Engine misfires

1 Check 2, 3, 5 and 7 in (a)
2 Weak contact breaker spring
3 HT plug or coil lead cracked or perished
4 Loose sparking plug
5 Sparking plug insulation cracked
6 Sparking plug gap incorrect
7 Ignition timing too far advanced

(c) Poor acceleration

1 Ignition retarded
2 Centrifugal advance weights seized
3 Centrifugal advance springs weak, broken or disconnected
4 Distributor clamp or mounting screw loose
5 Excessive contact points gap
6 Worn sparking plugs
7 Faulty vacuum unit or leaking pipe

NOTES

CHAPTER 4

THE COOLING SYSTEM

4:1 Description

The cooling system is pressurised and thermostatically controlled. Water circulation is assisted by a centrifugal pump which is mounted on the cylinder block, the pump being driven by the camshaft drive belt. Tensioning of this belt is carried out by moving the water pump on its mountings. The cooling fan is driven by an electric motor mounted in the radiator shroud, and is controlled by a thermal switch.

The water pump takes coolant from the bottom of the radiator and delivers it to the cylinder block from which it rises to the cylinder head. At normal operating temperatures, the thermostat is opened and the coolant returns to the top of the radiator. At lower temperatures, the thermostat is closed and the coolant bypasses the radiator and returns directly to the pump inlet. This provides a rapid warm-up.

Radiator installation details for earlier models are shown in **FIG 4:1**. Later models have a similar installation, but a light alloy radiator and a separate expansion tank are fitted, the latter located as shown in **FIG 4:2**.

4:2 Routine maintenance

The cooling system should be checked regularly for correct coolant level when the engine is cool. On later models topping up is carried out at the expansion tank only. On earlier models, topping up is carried out at the radiator filler in the normal manner. **Do not remove the filler cap from radiator or expansion tank when the engine is hot or coolant expansion may cause scalding as the pressure is released.** Also, on later models, when the coolant is hot a false level will be indicated in the expansion tank, the level only setting down when the system is cool.

On earlier models, remove the radiator cap and check that the coolant level is at the bottom of the filler neck. On later models, check that the coolant level is between the MAX and MIN marks on the expansion tank. Top up the level as necessary.

It is recommended that an antifreeze solution is maintained in the system all year round. Topping up should therefore be carried out with the correct mixture of antifreeze and water to avoid weakening the solution in use.

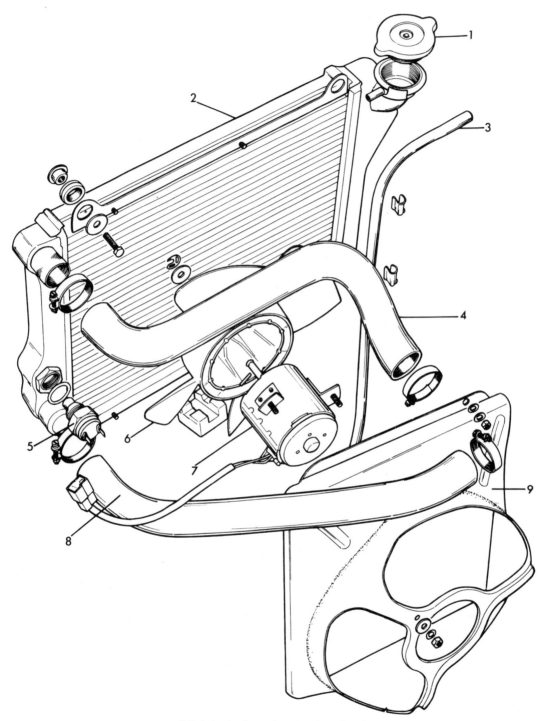

FIG 4:1   Radiator, hoses and cooling fan

Key to Fig 4:1   1 Radiator filler cap   2 Radiator   3 Overflow pipe   4 Top hose   5 Thermal switch   6 Cooling fan
7 Cooling fan motor   8 Bottom hose   9 Fan shroud

Every two years the cooling system should be drained, flushed to remove sediment and refilled with fresh antifreeze mixture. Check that the clips are tight on all hoses and that the radiator pressure cap and, if fitted, the expansion tank cap, is in good condition and sealing effectively. Loss of system pressure due to a leaking filler cap can be a cause of overheating.

Regular checks should be made on the condition and tension of the toothed belt, as described in **Chapter 1**.

Draining the system:

Open the heater control valve knob completely. Make sure that the system is cool. On models fitted with an expansion tank, remove the cap from the tank then remove the radiator cap. Remove the radiator cap on earlier models. Refer to **FIG 4:1**. Slacken the clip and remove bottom hose 8 from the radiator and allow the coolant to drain out. Remove the drain plug which is located on the side of the engine cylinder block beneath the exhaust manifold (see **FIG 4:3**).

Flushing:

When all old coolant has drained, reconnect the bottom hose and refit the drain plug. Fill the system with clean water through the radiator filler neck and run the engine until the top radiator hose feels warm, which indicates that the thermostat has opened for complete circulation. Now completely drain the system again before the sediment has time to settle.

Filling:

Check that the drain plug is properly fitted and that all hose clips are tight. Leave the heater control in the maximum heat position. Prepare the new antifreeze mixture according to the manufacturer's instructions. **If the system is still warm, allow it to cool down as adding the cold liquid when the system is warm may crack the engine cylinder block.** Open the cooling system bleed screw arrowed in **FIG 4:4**.

Slowly fill the system until the coolant level is at the bottom of the filler neck on the radiator, then tighten the bleed screw. Start the engine and allow it to run at idle speed until the cooling fan motor starts to run, which indicates that the system is at normal operating temperature. Top up to the correct level, refit the radiator cap and switch off the engine. On later models, fill the expansion bottle with coolant up to the MIN mark. Check the coolant level after running the engine for some time and top up if necessary. On later models, the level in the expansion tank should be maintained between the MIN and MAX marks.

4:3 The cooling fan

The cooling fan is electrically operated and switched on and off according to engine temperature by a thermal switch attached to the radiator. If the fan operates with the engine cold, the switch is faulty or there is a short-circuit in the fan wiring. If the fan does not operate at all, check the fuse, then check that the motor is in order by connecting jumper leads from the battery to the motor

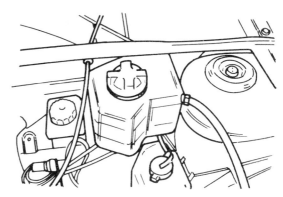

FIG 4:2   Cooling system expansion tank

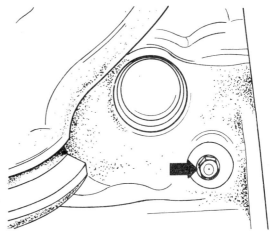

FIG 4:3   The cylinder block drain plug

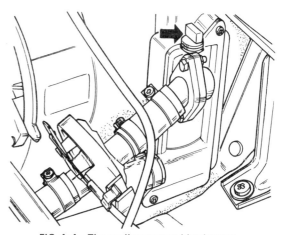

FIG 4:4   The cooling system bleed screw

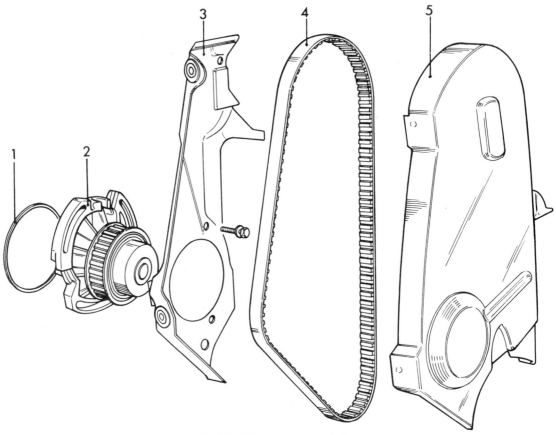

FIG 4:5 Water pump installation

Key to Fig 4:5   1 Sealing ring   2 Water pump assembly   3 Inner cover   4 Toothed belt   5 Outer cover

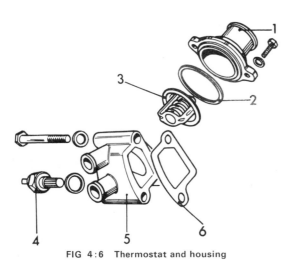

FIG 4:6 Thermostat and housing

Key to Fig 4:6 1 Top cover 2 Sealing ring 3 Thermostat
4 Temperature sensor   5 Thermostat housing   6 Gasket

terminals. If the motor is in order, check the wiring to the motor and thermal switch. If the wiring and connections are in order, suspect a faulty thermal switch.

The fan and motor assembly is removed complete with the air shroud as shown in **FIG 4:1**. Pull the wiring connector from the thermal switch. If the thermal switch is to be removed, drain the radiator first as described previously. Make sure that the sealing ring for the thermal switch is in good condition, renewing the ring if necessary.

4:4 Removing the radiator

Drain the cooling system as described in **Section 4:2**, there being no need to drain the cylinder block. Disconnect the electric fan motor wires at the thermal switch at the bottom of the radiator. Remove the fixing nuts and remove the fan, motor and shroud assembly from the rear of the radiator. Loosen the clip and disconnect the remaining radiator hose from the connection at the radiator. Remove the radiator fixing bolts and lift the radiator from the car.

Refit in the reverse order of removal. On completion, refill and bleed the cooling system as described in **Section 4:2**.

4:5 The water pump

Removal:

Refer to **Chapter 1** and remove the toothed belt from the crankshaft, camshaft and water pump pulleys. Drain the cooling system as described in **Section 4:2**. Unscrew the fixing bolts and remove inner cover 3, water pump assembly 2 and sealing ring 1 (see **FIG 4:5**).

The water pump is a sealed assembly, so it must be renewed complete if faulty.

Refitting:

Fit a new sealing ring between the pump and cylinder block if the original is not in perfect condition. Refit the water pump and inner cover, then fit and tension the toothed belt as described in **Chapter 1**, making sure that the timing marks are correctly aligned. On completion, refill and bleed the cooling system as described in **Section 4:2**.

4:6 The thermostat

The thermostat is fitted in a housing located between the cylinder head and radiator top hose, as shown in **FIG 4:6**.

Removal:

Drain sufficient coolant to bring the level below that of the thermostat assembly. Unscrew the fixing screws and detach the top cover 1 (see **FIG 4:6**). The top cover can remain attached to the radiator top hose. Remove sealing ring 2 and lift out thermostat 3.

Testing:

Clean the thermostat and immerse it in a container of cold water, together with a 0° to 100°C thermometer. Heat the water, keeping it stirred and check that the valve opens at approximately 85°C and is fully opened at approximately 100°C. The valve should close tightly when the thermostat is removed from the hot water and placed in cold water. If the thermostat operates correctly it may be refitted, but if not it must be renewed.

Refitting:

This is a reversal of the removal procedure. Use a new sealing ring if the original is not in perfect condition. On completion, refill and bleed the cooling system as described in **Section 4:2**.

4:7 Frost precautions

With the correct coolant solution in use as described in **Section 4:2**, no additional frost precautions should be necessary. However, it is advisable to have the solution tested at intervals during the winter to make certain that it has not weakened. A hydrometer calibrated to read both specific gravity and temperature for the type of coolant in the system must be used, most garages having such equipment. Always ensure that the antifreeze mixture used for filling the system is of sufficient strength to provide protection against freezing, according to the manufacturer's instructions.

4:8 Fault diagnosis

(a) Internal water leakage

1 Cracked cylinder wall
2 Loose cylinder head bolts
3 Cracked cylinder head
4 Faulty head gasket

(b) Poor circulation

1 Radiator core blocked
2 Engine water passages restricted
3 Low coolant level
4 Defective thermostat
5 Perished or collapsed radiator hoses

(c) Corrosion

1 Impurities in the coolant
2 Infrequent draining and flushing

(d) Overheating

1 Check (b)
2 Sludge in crankcase
3 Faulty ignition timing
4 Low oil level in sump
5 Tight engine
6 Choke exhaust system
7 Binding brakes
8 Slipping clutch
9 Incorrect valve timing
10 Weak fuel mixture

NOTES

CHAPTER 5

THE CLUTCH

5:1 Description

The clutch is a single dry plate unit of diaphragm spring type. The main components are the driven plate, pressure plate assembly and release bearing. The clutch assembly is interposed between the end of the engine crankshaft and the transmission assembly.

The driven plate consists of a resilient steel disc attached to a hub which slides on the splined transmission input shaft. The friction linings are riveted to both sides of the disc.

The pressure plate assembly consists of the pressure plate, diaphragm spring and housing, the assembly being bolted to the engine flywheel. The release bearing is a ballbearing of special construction with an elongated outer ring that presses directly against the diaphragm spring when the clutch pedal is operated. The bearing is mounted on a carrier and operated from a fork and pivot journaled in the transmission housing.

Clutch pedal movement is transmitted to the release bearing by a sheathed steel cable connected to the clutch release lever.

When the clutch is fully engaged, the driven plate is nipped between the pressure plate and the engine flywheel and transmits torque to the gearbox through the splined input shaft. When the clutch pedal is depressed, the pressure plate is withdrawn from the driven plate by force transmitted through the cable and the driven plate ceases to transmit torque to the gearbox.

5:2 Routine maintenance

Adjusting the clutch:

Clutch adjustment should be checked regularly as normal wear of the driven plate linings will alter the adjustment in service. If the cable is adjusted with insufficient free play, the cable will be tight and tend to prevent the clutch from engaging properly, causing slip and rapid clutch plate wear. If the cable has too much free play, the clutch will not release properly, causing drag and consequent poor gear change quality and difficulty in engaging gears from rest.

The clutch adjustment point at the end of the operating cable is shown in **FIG 5:1**. Clutch free play should be 15mm (0.590in) measured at the pedal pad. For accuracy, hold a ruler against the car floor and move the pedal by hand. If free play is not at the figure stated, turn the adjuster shown in **FIG 5:1** to correct.

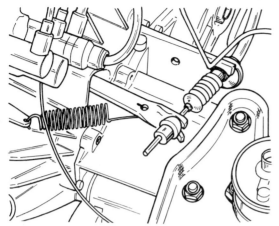

FIG 5:1 Clutch adjustment point at end of operating cable

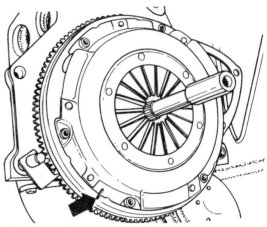

FIG 5:2 Removing and refitting clutch assembly

5:3 Removing and dismantling clutch

Remove the transmission as described in **Chapter 6**. Punch or scribe mark the clutch cover flange and flywheel rim, as shown in **FIG 5:2**, so that the clutch cover can be refitted to the flywheel in its original position. Lock the flywheel against rotation by suitable means. Fit tool 10-213, a spare transmission input shaft or a suitable mandrel through the clutch unit as shown in the illustra-tion. Loosen the clutch cover bolts alternately and evenly until clutch spring pressure has been released, then remove the screws completely. Lift off the clutch pressure plate and driven plate, taking care not to contaminate the driven plate linings with grease or oil. The pressure plate and driven plate are shown in **FIG 5:3**. Release the retaining clips and remove the release bearing from the release shaft as shown in **FIG 5:4**.

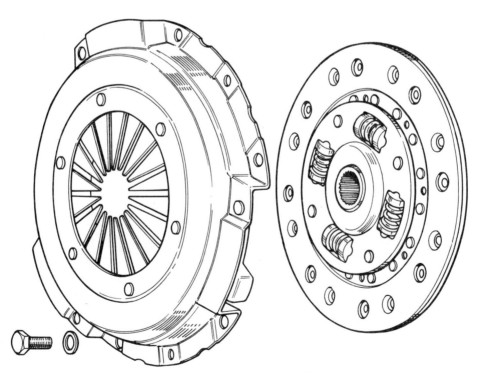

FIG 5:3 Clutch pressure plate assembly (left) and driven plate

Servicing:

Thoroughly clean all parts in a suitable solvent, with the exception of the driven plate linings and the release bearing. The release bearing must not be cleaned in solvent as this would wash the internal lubricant from the bearing.

The clutch cover, spring and pressure plate assembly is an integral unit and must not be dismantled. If any part is defective, the assembly must be renewed complete. Inspect the surface of the flywheel where the driven plate makes contact. Small cracks on the surface are unimportant, but if there are any deep scratches the flywheel should be machined smooth or renewed. Check the pressure plate for scoring or damage and check that the operating surface is flat and true. To do this, place a straightedge across the pressure plate assembly as shown in **FIG 5:5** and check any gap between straightedge and inner circumference using feeler gauges. Maximum allowable distortion is 0.3mm. Check the diaphragm spring for cracks or other damage and check that all rivets are tight. Check the release bearing for any roughness when it is pressed and turned by hand. Any parts which are worn or damaged must be renewed.

Check the driven plate for loose rivets and broken or very loose torsional springs. The friction linings should be well proud of the rivets and have a light colour with a polished glaze through which the grain of the material is clearly visible. A dark, glazed deposit indicates oil on the facings and, as this condition cannot be rectified, a new plate will be required. Any sign of oil in the clutch should be investigated as to the cause and rectified to prevent recurrence of the problem. Check the driven plate for distortion, preferably by mounting it between centres and using a dial gauge as shown in **FIG 5:6**. Run out at the circumference should not exceed 0.4mm. A slightly twisted driven plate can usually be corrected by mounting it on the splined shaft and using hand pressure to straighten it. More serious distortion will dictate fitting of a new plate. Check the driven plate hub for a smooth, sliding fit on the splined input shaft, removing any burrs on the shaft or in the hub.

5:4 Assembling and refitting clutch

Reassembly is a reversal of the dismantling procedure. Lightly coat the splines in the driven plate hub with Molykote powder. The driven plate hub must be centralised with the flywheel hub during assembly, using a spare transmission input shaft, tool 10-201 or other suitable mandrel as shown in **FIG 5:2**.

Place the driven plate correctly on the pressure plate and insert the alignment tool through both. Hold the complete assembly against the flywheel while inserting the end of the tool into the pilot bearing in the crankshaft. Index the alignment marks made during the dismantling procedure and install the clutch cover to flywheel attachments bolts finger tight. Complete tightening of the bolts alternately and evenly to a final torque of 25Nm (18lb ft). Remove the alignment tool. Refit the release bearing to the release shaft, lubricating the sliding surfaces sparingly with molybdenum disulphide grease. Refit the transmission as described in **Chapter 6** and adjust the clutch cable as described in **Section 5:2**.

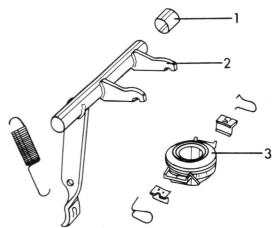

FIG 5:4 Clutch release bearing 3, shaft 2 and shaft bush 1

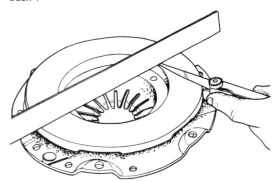

FIG 5:5 Checking pressure plate for distortion

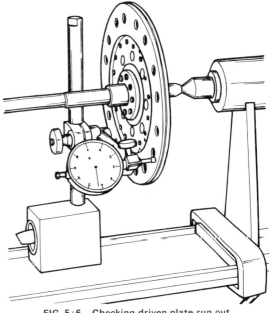

FIG 5:6 Checking driven plate run out

5:5 Fault diagnosis

(a) Drag or spin

1 Oil or grease on driven plate linings
2 Clutch cable binding
3 Distorted driven plate
4 Warped or damaged pressure plate
5 Broken driven plate linings
6 Excessive clutch free play

(b) Fierceness or snatch

1 Check 1, 2, 3 and 4 in (a)
2 Worn driven plate linings

(c) Slip

1 Check 1 in (a) and 2 in (b)
2 Weak diaphragm spring

3 Seized control cable
4 Insufficient clutch cable free play

(d) Judder

1 Check 1, 3 and 4 in (a)
2 Contact area of friction linings unevenly worn
3 Bent or worn splined shaft
4 Badly worn splines in driven plate hub
5 Faulty engine or transmission mountings

(e) Tick or knock

1 Badly worn driven plate hub splines
2 Worn release bearing
3 Bent or worn splined shaft
4 Loose flywheel

CHAPTER 6

THE TRANSMISSION

6:1 Description

A four-speed all syncromesh gearbox is fitted, gear operation being from the floor mounted gearlever. The gearbox assembly is fitted in line with the engine, across the car on the lefthand side, and incorporates the differential housing. The gearbox and differential components share the same oil supply. The oil level should be maintained at the bottom of the filler plug hole. Oil changes are not required as routine maintenance, it only being necessary to fill the transmission with new oil after overhaul procedures have been carried out.

Power from the engine crankshaft is transmitted through the clutch unit to the gearbox drive shaft. Power flow is then through the gears on the drive shaft and drive pinion to the differential, through the flanged drive shafts splined into the differential gears, then through the universally-jointed drive shafts which are splined into the front wheel hubs.

6:2 Gearchange linkage

Gearchange linkage adjustment must be carried out whenever the gear change linkage has been reconnected after servicing operations, or at any time when difficulty is experienced in gear selection.

Gearchange linkage adjustment:

Gearchange linkage components are shown in **FIG 6:1**. Set the gearlever in the neutral position, then slacken clamp nut 2. Raise the gearlever rubber boot, then install gauge 3003 as shown in **FIG 6:2**. Correctly align the base of the gearlever with the gauge, then tighten the clamp nut 2 to 21Nm (15 lb ft). Check that all gears can be selected smoothly and accurately.

Gearlever removal:

Slacken the clamp nut 2 shown in **FIG 6:1**. Raise the gearlever rubber boot, then remove the two nuts arrowed in **FIG 6:3** to release the gearlever assembly. Remove the assembly by sliding the selector rod in through the passenger compartment. Refit in the reverse order, adjusting the gearchange linkage as described previously. Lightly lubricate the pivot points shown at 6 in **FIG 6:1**.

6:3 Flanged shaft seals

The flanged shaft seals can be renewed without the need for transmission removal.

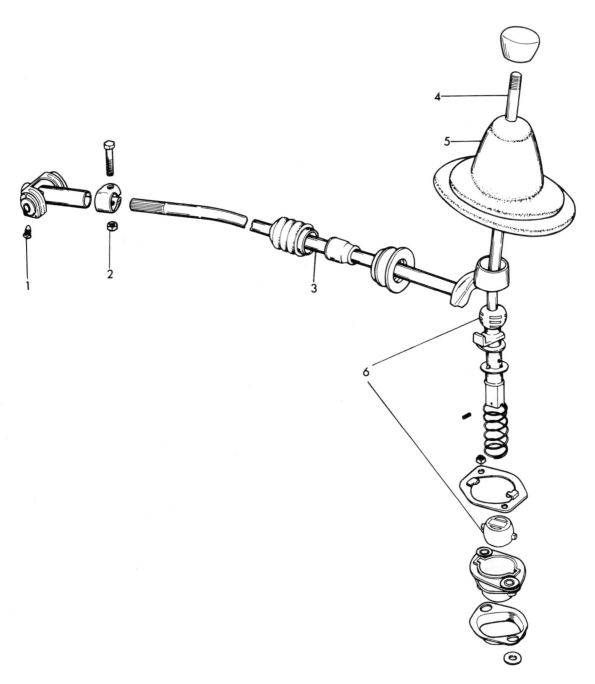

FIG 6:1   Gearchange linkage components

Key to Fig 6:1   1 Screw   2 Clamp nut   3 Selector rod   4 Gearlever   5 Rubber boot   6 Pivot points

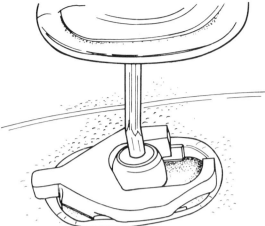

FIG 6:2 Aligning gearlever with the special gauge

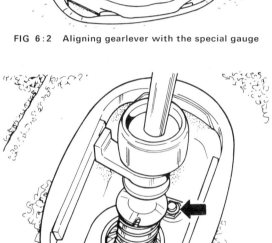

FIG 6:3 Gearlever removal

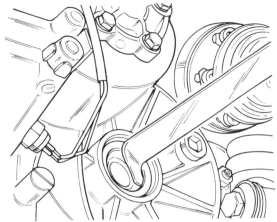

FIG 6:4 Removing flanged shaft seal

FIG 6:5 Lefthand seal (left) and righthand seal (right)

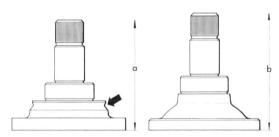

FIG 6:6 Lefthand (left) and righthand (right) flanged shafts. Dimension a = 84.5mm, dimension b = 89.5mm

Removal:

Refer to **Chapter 7** and detach the appropriate drive shaft at its inner end. Support the drive shaft with wire to avoid damage. Remove the central bolt and pull out the flanged shaft. Use a suitable hooked tool to remove the seal as shown in **FIG 6:4**, taking care not to damage the transmission case.

Note that lefthand and righthand flanged shafts and seals are different and care must be taken to install correctly. The lefthand seal has an interrupted groove around the outer circumference, the righthand seal has a continuous groove (see arrows in **FIG 6:5**). The arrow on the seal itself shows the direction of flanged shaft rotation. The flanged shafts are shown in **FIG 6:6**. The lefthand unit can be readily identified by the machined groove arrowed.

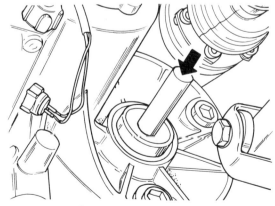

FIG 6:7 Installing flanged shaft seal

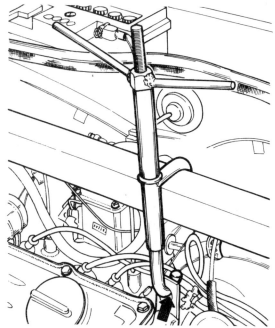

FIG 6:8 Supporting the engine with the special tool

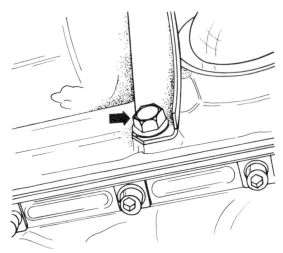

FIG 6:10 Inlet manifold support screw

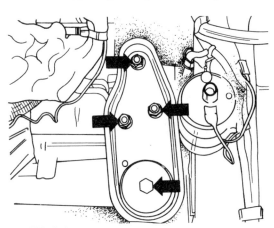

FIG 6:9 Lefthand engine mounting removal

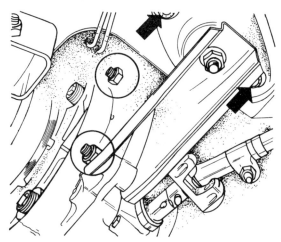

FIG 6:11 Rear engine mounting removal

Installation:

Fill the space between the lips on the new seal with multi-purpose grease, then drive the seal up to the stop using tool 2005 or similar as shown in **FIG 6:7**. Install the drive shaft and tighten the retaining bolt to 45Nm (32.5lb ft). On completion, check the transmission oil level.

6:4 Removing and refitting transmission

Removal:

If the transmission is to be dismantled, remove the transmission oil drain plug and collect the oil in a waste container. When all old oil has drained, wipe any metal particles from the magnetic drain plug then install and tighten to 25Nm (18 lb ft).

Remove the windscreen washer container. Support the weight of the engine with the special tool shown in **FIG 6:8**, or by installing suitable lifting equipment. Remove the lefthand engine mounting as shown in **FIG 6:9**. Refer to **Chapter 5** and disconnect the clutch cable from release lever and transmission. Remove the inlet manifold support screw arrowed in **FIG 6:10**, then loosen the screw at the manifold and turn the support to clear.

Refer to **Chapter 11** and remove the starter motor. Unscrew the clamps at the coolant pipe and remove the holder. Disconnect both drive shafts at their inner ends

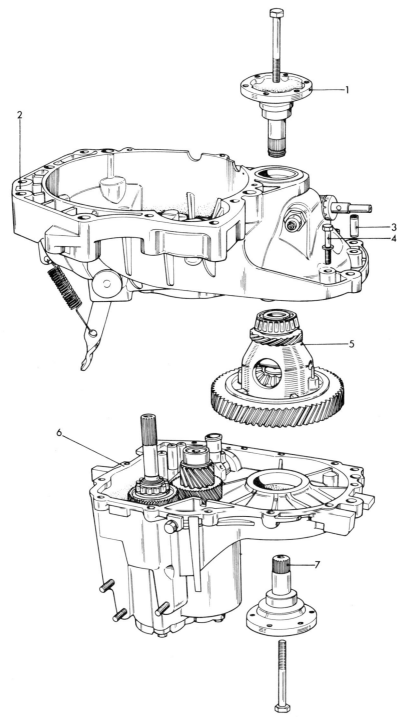

FIG 6:12   Bearing housing and differential assembly

Key to Fig 6:12   1 Righthand flanged shaft   2 Bearing housing   3 Dowel pin   4 Fixing screw   5 Differential assembly
6 Transmission case assembly   7 Lefthand flanged shaft

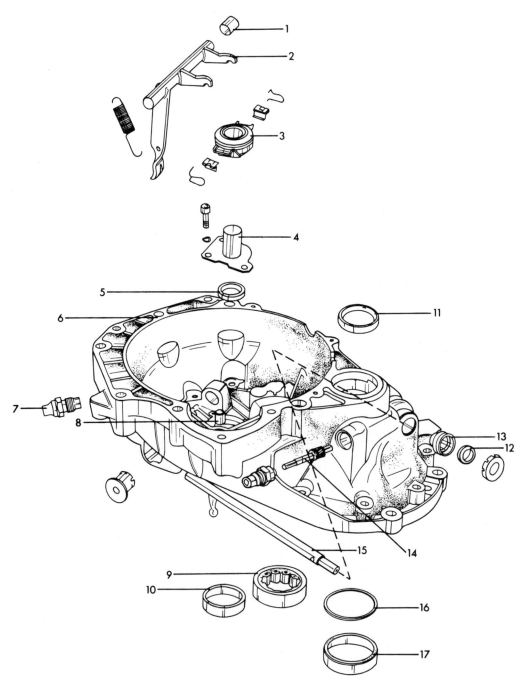

FIG 6:13 Bearing housing components

Key to Fig 6:13   1 Bearing bush   2 Release shaft   3 Release bearing   4 Guide sleeve   5 Drive shaft seal   6 Bearing housing   7 Transmitter   8 Starter bearing bush   9 Drive pinion bearing outer race   10 Drive shaft bearing outer race   11 Righthand flanged shaft seal   12 Inner selector lever seal   13 Inner selector lever bearing bush   14 Speedometer driven gear   15 Inner selector lever   16 Shim   17 Differential taper roller bearing outer race

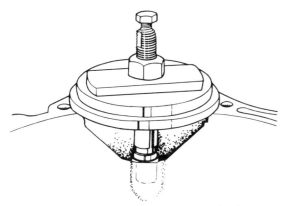

FIG 6:14 Removing starter bearing bush

(see **Chapter 7**). Disconnect the reversing lamp wire from the connector on the transmission. Unlock and remove the screw shown at 1 in **FIG 6:1**. Remove the rear engine mounting as shown in **FIG 6:11**. Disconnect the earth cable from the transmission.

Remove the flywheel guard. Remove the screws connecting the transmission to the engine. Support the transmission and carefully lever it away from the engine, then remove the transmission assembly from the vehicle.

Refitting:

This is a reversal of the removal procedure. Take care not to damage the drive shaft or clutch unit splines when mating the two components. When refitting the lefthand engine mounting, tighten the nuts shown by the upper arrows in **FIG 6:9** to 42Nm (30lb ft) and the bolt shown by the lower arrow to 55Nm (39.5 lb ft). When refitting the rear engine mounting, refer to **FIG 6:11** and tighten the arrowed fixings to 30Nm (21.5lb ft) and the circled fixings to 42Nm (30lb ft). Tighten the screw shown at 1 in **FIG 6:1** to 14Nm (10lb ft) and lock with a new piece of soft wire.

On completion, check gearchange linkage adjustment as described previously and clutch cable adjustment as described in **Chapter 5**. Check gearbox oil and top up to the correct level.

6:5 Transmission overhaul procedures

The transmission internal components are engineered to close tolerances and major overhaul procedures dictate very accurate resetting of components in relation to each other and to the transmission case. This work can only be satisfactorily carried out if the necessary special tools, measuring equipment and test facilities are available. For this reason, all major overhaul work should be entrusted to a fully equipped Volkswagen service station.

The important component settings concern the drive shaft, drive pinion and differential assembly. The drive shaft position must be adjusted if the drive shaft or its grooved ballbearing is renewed. The drive pinion position must be adjusted if the drive pinion, drive pinion ball-bearing or the thrust washer for first gear is renewed. The differential assembly must be adjusted if the bearing

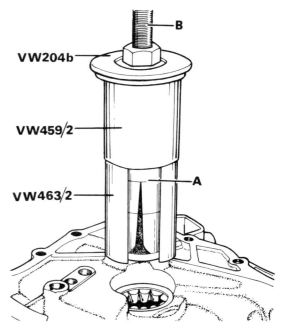

FIG 6:15 Removing drive shaft roller bearing outer race. (Use VW 295 and 295a when needle bearings are used.)

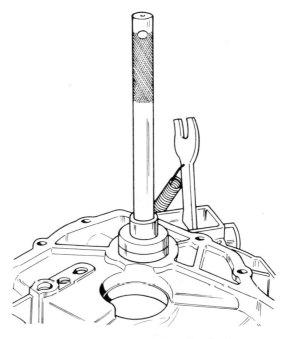

FIG 6:16 Installing drive shaft roller bearing outer race. With the latter needle type, the lettering on the bearing must face the drift

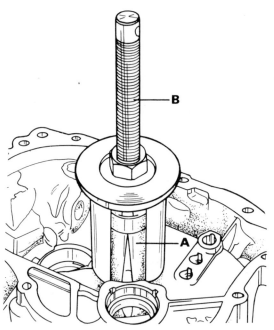

FIG 6:17 Removing drive pinion bearing outer race

housing, differential assembly or differential taper roller bearing is renewed. All three adjustment procedures must be carried out if a new transmission case is fitted. The vehicle should therefore be taken to a service station if work involving renewal of any of the components mentioned is required.

However, the transmission can be dismantled for component inspection by a fairly competent owner/mechanic, as described in this chapter. Note that even this work will require the use of a number of special tools, as noted in the accompanying text or illustrations, and the operator should check on the availability of these or suitable substitutes before starting the work.

6:6 Bearing housing and differential

Dismantling and servicing:

Remove the transmission assembly as described in **Section 6:4** and remove the flanged shafts as described in **Section 6:3**. Thoroughly clean the outside of the transmission assembly to avoid the entry of dirt during dismantling. Refer to **FIG 6:12**.

Mount the transmission on an assembly stand or support on suitable wooden blocks with the bearing housing uppermost. Remove the 13 screws shown at 4 in **FIG 6:12** and detach the bearing housing from the transmission case. Collect the two dowel pins 3 if they are loosened during removal. Lift out differential assembly 5. Examine the bearing housing 2 and differential assembly 5 for any signs of wear or damage. If the bearing housing casting or any differential assembly components need to be renewed, the work must be carried out by a fully equipped service station. This also applies if the taper roller bearing outer race shown at 17 in

FIG 6:13 is to be renewed. Otherwise, the bearing housing components can be serviced as described in the following paragraphs.

Refer to **FIG 6:13**. Remove release shaft 2, release bearing 3 and guide sleeve 4. If bearing bush 1 is worn, drive out with a suitable mandrel and drive in a new bush until it is flush with the housing. Instructions for servicing the release bearing will be found in **Chapter 5**.

Renew flanged shaft seal 11 as described in **Section 6:3**. Carefully lever out selector lever seal 12. If bush 13 is worn, drive out selector lever 15 then drive out the bush with a suitable mandrel. Drive in a new bush then refit the

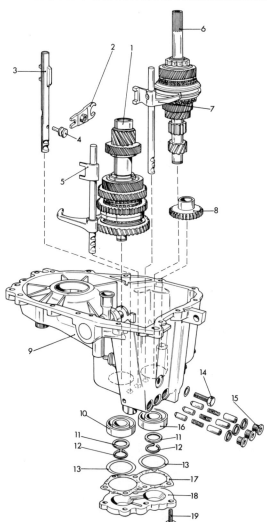

FIG 6:18 Drive shaft and drive pinion components

Key to Fig 6:18 1 Drive pinion assembly 2 Reverse lever 3 Reverse selector rod 4 Reverse lever guide pin 5 First and second gear selector rod and fork 6 Drive shaft assembly 7 Third and fourth gear selector rod and fork 8 Reverse gear 9 Transmission case 10 Drive pinion grooved ballbearing 11 Small shim 12 Circlip 13 Large shim 14 Screw 15 Selector detent plug 16 Drive shaft grooved ballbearing 17 Gasket 18 Bearing cover 19 Screw

inner selector lever. Fill the lips of a new seal 12 with multi-purpose grease, then drive the seal squarely into place.

If starter bearing bush 8 is worn, use the tools shown in **FIG 6 : 14** to pull out the bush. Use a suitable mandrel to drive the new bush into position until it is flush with the housing.

Remove drive shaft seal 5 (see **FIG 6 : 13**). Fill the space between the lips of a new seal with multi-purpose grease then press squarely into position.

Use Kukko tools 21/6 (A) and 22/2 (B) in conjunction with the VW tools shown in **FIG 6 : 15**, to remove the drive shaft roller bearing outer race. Note that later models have needle bearings with no inner race. Spread arms of inner extractor in the groove between the collar and outer race bearing surface. Drive a new bearing outer race into position, with closed end of bearing cage towards bearing housing, as shown in **FIG 6 : 16**. Renew drive pinion bearing outer race (9 in **FIG 6 : 13**) in a similar manner, removing with Kukko 21/5 and 22/2 and VW tools as shown in **FIG 6 : 17**. Install new bearing, with closed end of bearing cage towards bearing housing, using tools VW 295 and VW 554 or 512 (needle bearing). With the needle bearing the lettering must face the drift.

As the needle bearings have no inner race, the seats have been enlarged in diameter and the drive shaft oil seal has been altered accordingly. The new seal can be identified by six indented marks on its outer face.

If necessary, remove speedometer driven gear 14 (see **FIG 6 : 13**) by unscrewing the bearing plug.

Reassembly:

This is a reversal of the dismantling procedure, noting the following points:

Carefully clean the mating surfaces of bearing housing and transmission case and apply a coat of VW Sealant D3 to these surfaces before fitting bearing housing to case. Install screws shown at 4 in **FIG 6 : 12** finger tight, then tighten alternately and evenly to 25Nm (18lb ft). Lubricate all bearings and bushes with the correct grade of transmission oil, with the exception of clutch release components shown at 1, 2, 3 and 4 in **FIG 6 : 13** which should be lightly smeared with Molybdenum Disulphide paste.

6 : 7 Drive shaft and drive pinion

Separate the bearing housing and transmission case as described in **Section 6 : 6**. The drive shaft can be removed and installed alone, but if the drive pinion is to be removed the drive shaft must be removed first. Both shaft and pinion must be removed before the reverse gear can be removed. The components are shown in **FIG 6 : 18**.

Take care to keep ballbearings 10 and 16 and shims 11 and 13 in the correct order for refitting in their original positions. If ballbearings or shims are mixed, or if either ballbearing is renewed, drive pinion and drive shaft adjustments must be carried out after reassembly, this being a specialist job.

Drive shaft removal:

Unscrew the plugs and remove selector detent mechanism and springs (see 15 in **FIG 6 : 18**). Remove

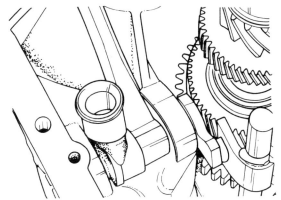

FIG 6 : 19   Clamping selector shaft

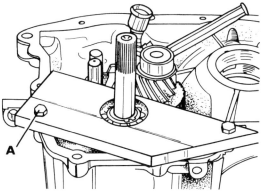

FIG 6 : 20   Installing support 2011

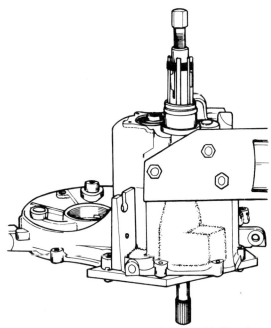

FIG 6 : 21   Removing drive shaft grooved ballbearing

the fixing screws and detach bearing cover 18. Discard gasket 17 as a new one must be fitted during reassembly. Keep large bearing shims 13 in the correct order. Remove screw 14 and remove reverse selector rod 3 with guide pin 4 and reverse lever 2.

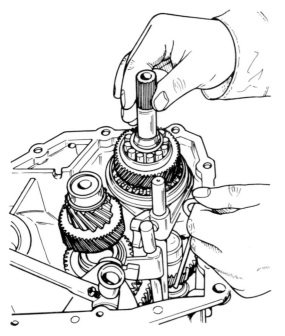

FIG 6:22 Removing drive shaft

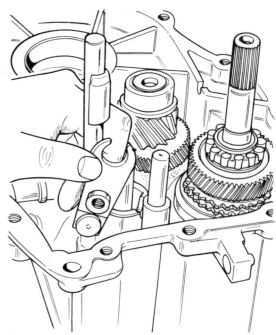

FIG 6:24 Installing reverse selector mechanism

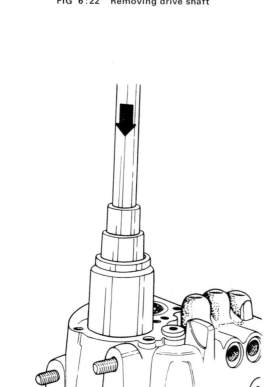

FIG 6:23 Driving in drive shaft grooved ballbearing

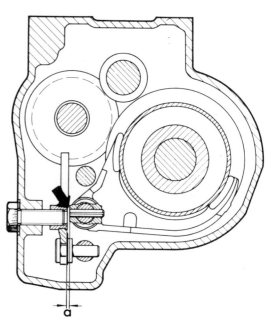

FIG 6:25 Installing reverse lever screw

Use a chisel or similar tool to clamp the selector shaft as shown in **FIG 6:19**. Refer to **FIG 6:20** and install support 2011 with two M8 × 25 screws (A). Remove circlip and small shim for drive shaft ballbearing. Remove the ballbearing as shown in **FIG 6:21**, then remove the support. Remove drive shaft with third and fourth gear selector rod and selector fork, lifting reverse gear slightly with a wire hook as shown in **FIG 6:22**.

If the drive shaft or any associated component is to be renewed, the work should be carried out by a service station having the necessary special tools and equipment.

Refitting:

Lubricate all parts with the correct grade of hypoid gear oil when refitting. Install complete drive shaft with third and fourth gear selector rod and selector fork, lifting reverse gear slightly with a wire hook as shown in **FIG 6:22**. Make sure that the locks 1 for the selector mechanism are correctly positioned (see **FIG 6:31** and **Section 6:8**).

Install support 2011 then drive in the grooved ball-bearing. When installed, the closed end of the ballbearing cage faces towards the transmission case. Install the small shim and circlip, then remove the support. Drive the grooved ballbearing fully against the stop in the housing as shown in **FIG 6:23**.

Install reverse selector rod with guide pin and reverse lever, as shown in **FIG 6:24**. Let reverse lever rest on reverse gear, turn selector rod to the right and swing in the reverse lever. Make sure that the key is flush in the selector fork.

Install the screw shown at 14 in **FIG 6:18** so that the play between reverse lever and first and second gear selector fork shown at a in **FIG 6:25** is 1.3 to 2.8mm. The screw should be tightened to 35Nm (25lb ft). Install large shim for drive shaft ballbearing, fit a new gasket and replace the ballbearing cover. Tighten the cover fixing screws to 25Nm (18lb ft). Install the selector detent mechanism correctly (see **FIG 6:31** and **Section 6:8**). Test gear change operation before reassembling further. It should be possible to shift into all gears easily. The selector detent mechanism should prevent selector rods located next to each other from shifting at the same time.

Refit the bearing housing to the transmission case as described in **Section 6:6**.

Drive pinion removal:

Remove the drive shaft as described previously. Remove the circlip and small shim for drive pinion (see **FIG 6:18**). Do not mix drive shaft and drive pinion shims. Press out the drive pinion together with first and second gear selector rod, selector fork and reverse gear. This operation is carried out in the same manner as that for drive shaft ballbearing removal, using tool 30-207 as shown in **FIG 6:21**.

If the drive pinion or any associated component is to be renewed, the work should be carried out by a specialist service station.

Refitting:

Install the grooved ballbearing, making sure that the closed end of the bearing cage faces towards the transmission case. Press the bearing fully home as shown

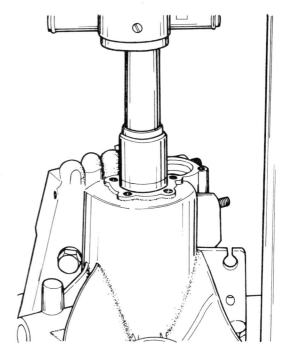

FIG 6:26 Installing drive pinion grooved ballbearing

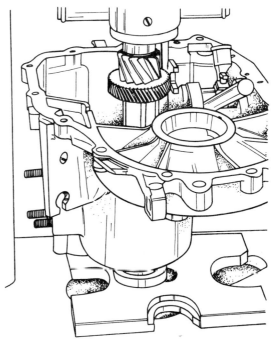

FIG 6:27 Drive pinion installation

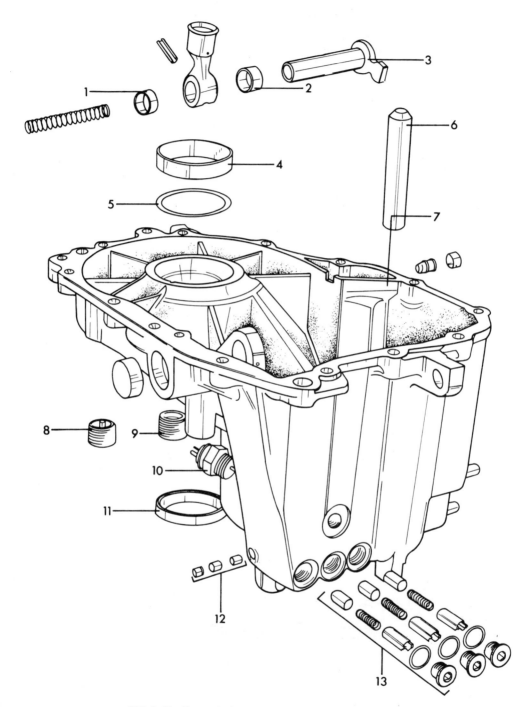

FIG 6:28 Transmission case and associated components

Key to Fig 6:28   1 Outer selector shaft bearing bush   2 Inner selector shaft bearing bush   3 Selector shaft   4 Differential taper roller bearing outer race   5 Shim   6 Reverse gear shaft   7 Transmission case   8 Magnetic oil drain plug   9 Oil filler plug   10 Reversing light switch   11 Lefthand flanged shaft seal   12 Detent locks   13 Detent bushes, springs, sleeves, washers and plugs

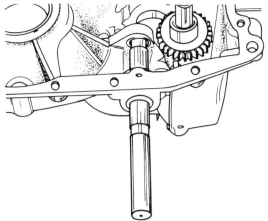

FIG 6:29 Removing selector shaft bush

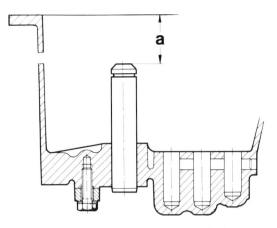

FIG 6:30 Reverse gear shaft installation

in **FIG 6:26**. Install complete drive pinion with first and second gear selector rod and selector fork as well as reverse gear. Make sure that the selector detent locks are correctly positioned (see **FIG 6:31** and **Section 6:8**). Press drive pinion fully home as shown in **FIG 6:27**. Install small shim and circlip for drive pinion. Refit the drive shaft assembly as described previously.

6:8 Transmission case and selector mechanism

Transmission case and associated components are shown in **FIG 6:28**. Note that if the differential taper roller bearing outer race or the transmission case itself are to be renewed, the work should be carried out only by a specialist service station (see **Section 6:5**).

Remove the drive shaft and drive pinion assemblies, if necessary for access to inner transmission case components.

Renewal of the flanged shaft seal is described in **Section 6:3**. If the selector shaft bearing bushes are worn, drive them out with a suitable mandrel as shown in **FIG 6:29**. Drive the new bushes into place until they are flush with the case. Note that the bushes are different

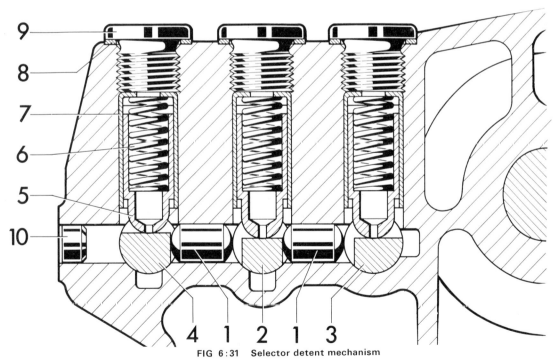

FIG 6:31 Selector detent mechanism

Key to Fig 6:31 1 Locks selector rod 2 First and second gear selector rod 3 Third and fourth gear selector rod 4 Reverse gear selector rod 5 Detent bush 6 Detent spring 7 Guide sleeve 8 Washer 9 Screw plug 10 Plug

lengths, the outer bush 1 being 9mm long, the inner bush 2 being 14mm long.

If the reverse gear shaft 6 is to be renewed, drive the shaft from the transmission case. The new shaft should be coated with VW D6 fluid before installation. Install the shaft until dimension a in **FIG 6 : 30** is 80.2 ± 0.3 mm.

Selector detent mechanism:

The selector detent mechanism is shown at 12 and 13 in **FIG 6 : 28** and a section through the assembly is shown in **FIG 6 : 31**. The bushes 5, under pressure from springs 6 engage with grooves in the selector rods to positively lock each gear as it is selected. The locks 1 also engage with grooves in the selector rods. When one selector rod is moved to engage a gear, the locks move in their bores to engage with the other two rods and prevent them from moving.

The selector detent mechanism must be correctly installed during transmission reassembly. The components are numbered in **FIG 6 : 31** in the correct order for installation. All parts should be lubricated with the correct grade of hypoid transmission oil during installation. Locks 1 should be correctly located in their bores first, then selector rod 2 with selector fork and complete drive pinion must be installed. Selector rod 3 is then fitted, with selector fork and complete drive pinion. Reverse gear selector rod 4 is then fitted, with reverse lever and guide pin. Installation of the drive shaft, drive pinion and selector rods is described in **Section 6 : 7**. With the selector rods and locks correctly installed, fit the bushes 5, springs 6, guide sleeves 7 and plugs 9. Finally, install plug 10.

Lubricate all gears and shafts with the correct grade of hypoid gear oil, before reassembling the transmission as described previously.

6 : 8 Fault diagnosis

(a) Jumping out of gear

1 Excessively worn selector rods
2 Worn syncromesh assemblies
3 Loose or worn selector fork
4 Selector detents incorrectly installed
5 Detent springs weak or broken

(b) Noisy transmission

1 Insufficient or dirty oil
2 Bearings worn or damaged
3 Worn drive shaft joints
4 Worn syncromesh units

(c) Difficulty in engaging gear

1 Incorrect clutch adjustment
2 Worn syncromesh assemblies
3 Worn selector rods or forks
4 Incorrect selector linkage adjustment

(d) Oil leaks

1 Damaged joint washers or gaskets
2 Worn or damaged oil seals
3 Faulty joint faces on transmission case components

CHAPTER 7

FRONT SUSPENSION AND DRIVE SHAFTS

7:1 Description
7:2 Coil springs and dampers
7:3 Steering knuckles
7:4 Control arms

7:5 Anti-roll bar
7:6 Drive shafts
7:7 Front wheel geometry
7:8 Fault diagnosis

7:1 Description

Independent front wheel suspension is by means of helically coiled springs controlled by double-acting hydraulic telescopic dampers. The damper units also act as pivots for the front wheel hub assemblies to accommodate steering movement. The suspension springs are fitted co-axially to the damper struts between two pressed steel support cups. **FIG 7:1** shows front suspension components.

The front wheel hubs are splined to the outer ends of the drive shafts and are carried on single wide ballbearing units fitted at each steering knuckle assembly.

The steering knuckle assemblies are located at the upper points by the damper unit attachments and at the lower points by short control arms. Additional location is provided by the anti-roll bar which connects between the outer ends of the control arms and is journaled at the front of the car body. Ball joints are used at the control arm to steering knuckle connections to accommodate movement during suspension travel. All joints and pivots in the front suspension are lubricated for life, no maintenance being required.

Note that certain special tools will be needed in order to carry out some of the overhaul work described in this

chapter and the owner would be well advised to check on the availability of these factory tools or suitable substitutes before tackling the items involved.

7:2 Coil springs and dampers

Removal:

Use a screwdriver to lever the plastic cap from the road wheel. Slacken the wheel bolts, then raise and safely support the front of the car on stands placed beneath body members. Unscrew the collared nut shown at 4 in **FIG 7:1**, then remove the road wheel and detach the nut and washer. Remove nut 3 then detach the tie rod ball joint from the arm on the suspension strut, using a suitable puller as shown in **FIG 7:2**.

Remove the bolts arrowed in **FIG 7:3** and detach the brake caliper. Wire the caliper to the brake pipe bracket so that the hose is not strained. Do not touch the brake pedal while the caliper is removed. Loosen the clamp bolt indicated by the lower arrow in **FIG 7:3**.

Use a suitable jack to take the tension of the anti-roll bar, then disconnect the righthand anti-roll bar mounting as described in **Section 7:5** and lower the jack. This releases the anti-roll bar tension.

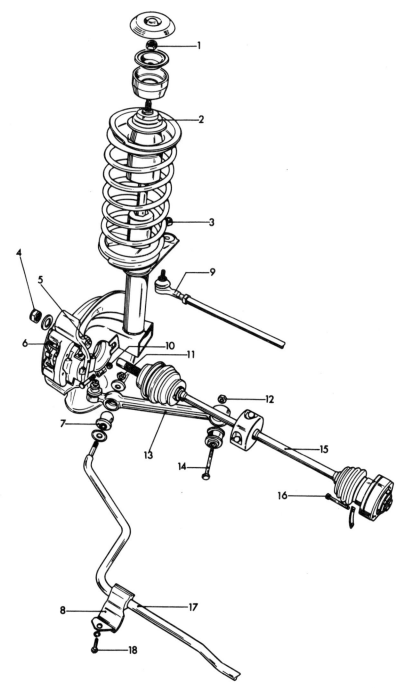

FIG 7:1 Layout of front suspension components

Key to Fig 7:1   1 Upper attachment nut   2 Coil spring assembly   3 Ball joint nut   4 Drive shaft nut   5 Caliper fixing bolt   6 Caliper   7 Bush   8 Anti-roll bar mounting   9 Tie rod   10, 11, 12 Fixing nuts   13 Control arm   14 Pivot bolt   15 Drive shaft   16 Fixing bolt   17 Anti-roll bar   18 Screw

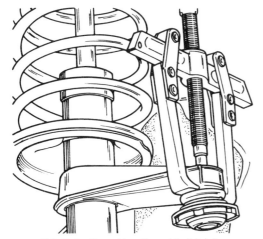

FIG 7:2 Detaching tie rod ball joint

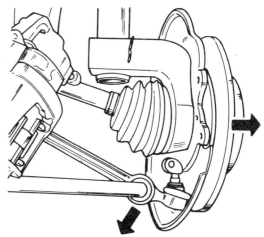

FIG 7:5 Detaching steering knuckle from ball joint and drive shaft

Remove the control arm inner pivot bolt and the coupling clamping bolt as shown in **FIG 7:4**. Pull down hard on the anti-roll bar and control arm to disconnect the lower ball joint from the steering knuckle. Spring the suspension strut assembly outwards to disconnect the knuckle assembly from the end of the drive shaft (see **FIG 7:5**). Tie the drive shaft to the body to prevent damage. From inside the engine compartment, remove the cover and unscrew the upper fixing nut shown at 1 in **FIG 7:1**. Remove the suspension and steering knuckle unit from the car.

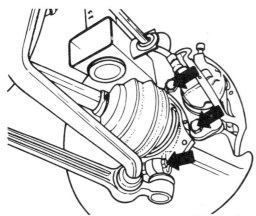

FIG 7:3 Caliper mounting bolts and ball joint clamp bolt

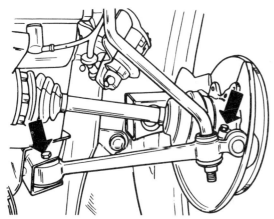

FIG 7:4 Control arm pivot bolt and coupling clamp bolt

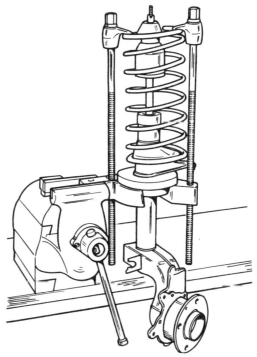

FIG 7:6 Compressing coil spring

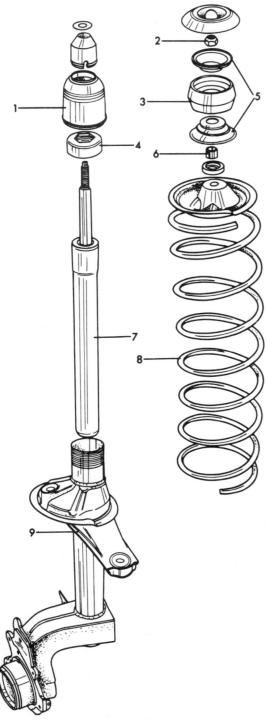

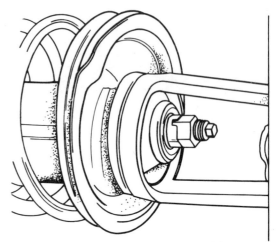

FIG 7:8   Upper cap nut tool in position

Dismantling coil spring and damper:

To remove and refit a coil spring it is essential to use a spring compressor tool, as shown in **FIG 7:6**. **FIG 7:7** shows coil spring and damper components. With the spring compressed, remove upper cap nut 6, using tool 3001 as shown in **FIG 7:8**. Push the tool over the threads and engage with the cap nut, then unscrew tool and nut with a spanner. Evenly release the spring compressor, then remove the coil spring assembly from the suspension strut. Note that the spring compressor in use in **FIG 7:8** is an alternative type to that shown in **FIG 7:6**.

If the damper unit is to be removed, unscrew the lower cap nut with tool 40-201 as shown in **FIG 7:9**. Note that, on factory installed damper units, some oil will escape from the damper housing during dismantling. New damper units are sealed assemblies, so the original piston rod, guide ring and hydraulic oil must be removed from the tube. To remove a damper unit from the tube, screw a nut to the top of the piston rod and tap upwards with a hammer against a spanner beneath the nut, as shown in **FIG 7:10**. Carefully guide a new damper into the tube and push in hard. Never use a hammer to install a damper unit. Tighten the lower cap nut to 140Nm (101lb ft).

Refit the coil spring using the compressor tool shown in **FIG 7:6**. Tighten the upper cap nut to 50Nm (36lb ft).

Refitting:

This is a reversal of the removal procedure, noting the following points:

Guide the drive shaft and shaft coupling into the steering knuckle and fit the screws. Secure the upper control arm, then reconnect the anti-roll bar righthand bearing as described in **Section 7:5**. Tighten the fixings shown in **FIG 7:1** as follows: Nut 3 to 37Nm (27lb ft), caliper fixing bolts 5 to 57Nm (41lb ft), nut 10 to 30Nm (21.5lb ft), nut 11 to 76Nm (55lb ft), nut 12 to 62Nm (45lb ft) and screws 18 to 30Nm (21.5lb ft). Always use a **new** nut 4, tightened to 210Nm (152lb ft), and a **new** nut 1, tightened to 50Nm (36lb ft). On completion, front wheel geometry should be checked as described in **Section 7:7**.

FIG 7:7   Coil spring and damper components

Key to Fig 7:7   1 Cover   2 Upper fixing nut   3 Insulator
4 Lower cap nut   5 Cups   6 Upper cap nut   7 Damper
unit   8 Coil spring   9 Steering knuckle assembly

7:3 Steering knuckles

Steering knuckle removal is carried out complete with coil spring and damper assembly as described in **Section 7:2**, but it is not necessary to remove the coil spring in order to overhaul the steering knuckle assembly. Dismantling and reassembling the knuckle requires press equipment. For each operation a suitable support plate and press tools of the appropriate diameter are necessary.

Dismantling:

FIG 7:11 shows steering knuckle components. Remove screws 2 and detach brake disc from wheel hub. Remove screws 3 and detach shield 5 from the steering knuckle.

The wheel hub must be pressed from the steering knuckle as shown in **FIG 7:12**. Extract the bearing inner race from the wheel hub, using a suitable puller in conjunction with tool 3002 as shown in **FIG 7:13**.

Remove inner and outer circlips shown at 6 and 8 in **FIG 7:11**. Press the bearing from the steering knuckle as shown in **FIG 7:14**.

Reassembly:

Fit the outer circlip into the groove, then press in a new bearing up to the circlip using the tools shown in **FIG 7:14**. Fit the inner circlip. Fit the steering knuckle assembly over the wheel hub, then press the knuckle on to the hub as shown in **FIG 7:15**. Note that the press tool should only rest on the inner bearing race when pressed down.

Refit the steering knuckle and coil spring assembly to the car as described in **Section 7:2**.

7:4 Control arms

Removal:

To remove a control arm, raise the front of the car and safely support on floor stands placed beneath body members. Raise a jack beneath the centre of the anti-roll bar to take the tension, then remove the righthand anti-roll bar mounting. Remove the control arm pivot bolt and the ball joint clamping bolt arrowed in **FIG 7:4**, then pull down on the outer end of the control arm and anti-roll bar to disconnect the ball joint from the steering knuckle. Disconnect the control arm from the end of the anti-roll bar.

Renewing bushes:

For bush removal and refitting, the control arm must be supported on sleeve VW 519 and plate VW 401 as shown in **FIG 7:16**. Tool VW 411 shown in the illustration is used to remove the outer bush. To press in a new outer bush, use tools VW 412 and VW 248 in conjunction with the support tools previously mentioned. To remove an inner rubber bush, support with the same tools and press out with VW 412 and VW 421. Press in a new inner bush using tools VW 412 and VW 542 with the same support tools. In all cases, bushes will be easier to install if they are lubricated with soapy water.

Refitting:

This is a reversal of the removal procedure. Refit the anti-roll bar righthand mounting as described in **Section**

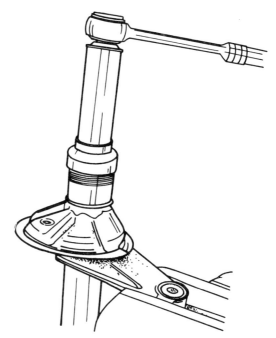

FIG 7:9   Removing lower cap nut

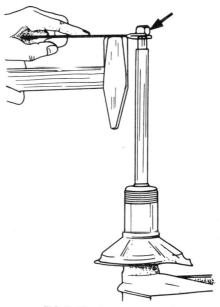

FIG 7:10   Damper removal

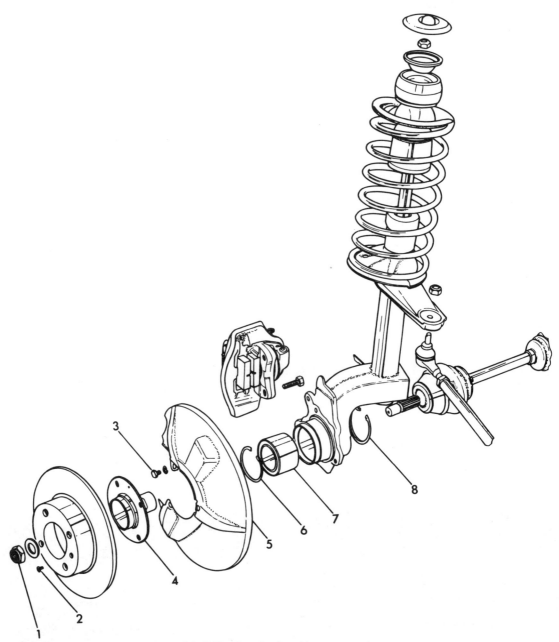

FIG 7:11   Steering knuckle components

Key to Fig 7:11   1 Drive shaft nut   2 Disc attachment screw   3 Shield attachment screw   4 Wheel hub   5 Shield
6 Outer circlip   7 Wheel bearing   8 Inner circlip

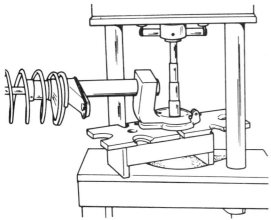

FIG 7:12   Removing wheel hub from steering knuckle

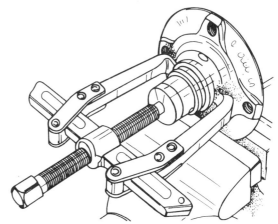

FIG 7:13   Removing bearing inner race

7:5. Tighten nut 10 to 30Nm (21.5lb ft), nut 11 to 76Nm (55lb ft) and nut 12 to 62Nm (45lb ft). The fixings are shown in **FIG 7:1**.

7:5 Anti-roll bar

Removal:

Use a suitable jack raised beneath the centre of the anti-roll bar to relieve its tension, as shown by the lefthand arrow in **FIG 7:17**. Remove the screws from the anti-roll bar mountings on each side. Remove the nuts securing the ends of the anti-roll bar to the control arms on each side, then drive out the ends of the bar using a soft-faced hammer.

Refitting:

With the help of an assistant, guide the ends of the anti-roll bar into the control arm bushes. Tighten the fixing nuts (11 in **FIG 7:1**) to 76Nm (55lb ft). Raise the centre of the anti-roll bar with a jack, then hold the mounting with pliers as shown in **FIG 7:17** while fitting the attachment screws. Tighten the screws (18 in **FIG 7:1**) to 30Nm (21.5lb ft).

7:6 Drive shafts

Removal:

With the car weight resting on the road wheels, remove the nut shown at 4 in **FIG 7:1**. Using a hexagon wrench of the correct size, remove the bolts securing the shaft inner flanges as shown in **FIG 7:18**. Turn the steering to full lock to improve access then, with the help of an assistant, press down on the front of the car body to compress the road spring until the drive shaft is loosened from the flanged shaft at the transmission. Now raise and safely support the car and pull the drive shaft from the steering knuckle as shown in **FIG 7:19**.

Servicing universal joints:

Overhaul of the inner and outer universal joints on the drive shafts is a specialist job, so it is recommended that all overhaul and repair procedures be entrusted to a fully equipped Volkswagen service station.

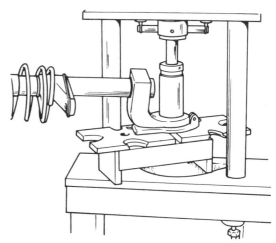

FIG 7:14   Removing and installing wheel bearing

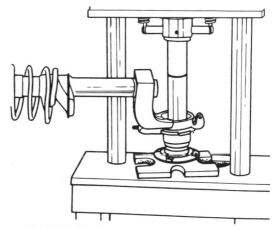

FIG 7:15   Fitting steering knuckle to wheel hub

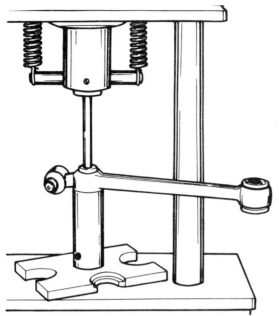

FIG 7:16   Control arm bush renewal

FIG 7:18   Removing drive shaft inner flange bolts

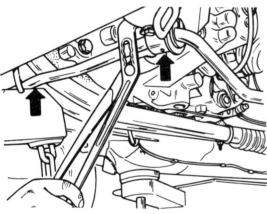

FIG 7:17   Anti-roll bar removal

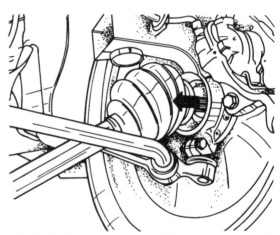

FIG 7:19   Removing drive shaft from steering knuckle

Refitting:

Insert the outer end of the drive shaft into the steering knuckle and fit the washer and a **new** retaining nut. With the steering turned to full lock, load the car to compress the road spring, then align the drive shaft to the transmission flange and fit the retaining bolts. Tighten these bolts to 40Nm (29lb ft) and the new outer drive shaft nut to 210Nm (152lb ft).

7:7 Front wheel geometry

Whenever suspension components have been dismantled or at any time when uneven tyre wear has been noted, the front suspension setting angles should be checked. Front wheel alignment should also be checked, this operation being described in **Chapter 9**. The correct setting angles are given in **Technical Data** in the

Appendix. The checking of front suspension angles should be carried out at a service station having special optical measuring equipment. Note that suspension geometry is not adjustable, so if any of the settings are found to be incorrect a check must be made for worn or damaged suspension components.

7:8 Fault diagnosis

(a) Wheel wobble

1 Worn hub bearings
2 Broken or weak front spring
3 Uneven tyre wear
4 Worn suspension linkage
5 Loose wheel fixings
6 Incorrect front wheel alignment

(b) Bottoming of suspension

1 Check 2 in (a)
2 Dampers ineffective
3 Car overloaded

(c) Heavy steering

1 Defective suspension struts
2 Incorrect suspension geometry

(d) Excessive tyre wear

1 Check 4 and 6 in (a) and 2 in (c)

(e) Rattles

1 Check 2 in (a) and 1 in (c)
2 Worn bushes
3 Loose components fixings

(f) Excessive rolling

1 Check 2 in (a) and 2 in (b)

NOTES

CHAPTER 8

REAR SUSPENSION AND HUBS

8:1 Description

Rear wheel suspension consists of fabricated steel trailing arms, joined by a torsion beam. Suspension movement is against helically coiled springs and controlled by vertical hydraulic telescopic dampers (see **FIG 8:1**). The rear wheel hubs are integral with the brake drums and each is carried on two taper roller bearings.

8:2 Rear hubs

Adjustment:

To check rear wheel hub adjustment, raise and safely support the rear of the car and remove the road wheel. Carefully lever off grease cap 2 (see **FIG 8:2**). The washer fitted behind the hub securing nut 3 should be free enough to be moved with the tip of a screwdriver as shown in **FIG 8:3**, without using leverage or excessive force.

If adjustment is required, remove the splitpin shown at 1 in **FIG 8:2** and remove the lock cap from the nut. Carefully adjust the nut until the correct freedom of movement is obtained at the washer. Spin the drum and hub assembly a few times during the adjustment to settle the bearings. If noise or roughness is apparent when adjustment is correct and the hub is turned by hand, the wheel bearings should be examined for wear or damage as described later.

When the adjustment is correct, fit the locking cap and secure with a new splitpin. Carefully tap the grease cap into place.

Wheel bearing removal:

Raise and safely support the rear of the car then remove the road wheel. Refer to **FIG 8:2**. Carefully lever off grease cap 2, then remove splitpin 1 and detach locking cap, nut 3 and washer. Pull the brake drum and hub from the stub axle, slackening off the rear brake adjuster as described in **Chapter 10** if the brake shoes bind against the drum. Carefully lever off seal 6 and remove inner and outer taper roller bearings 4 and 5.

Clean away the bearing grease and wash all parts in a suitable solvent and allow to dry. Lubricate the taper roller bearings with light oil and press them lightly into their outer races with the fingers. Check for roughness or noise when the bearings are gently pressed and turned. Check the outer races for wear or scoring. If any bearing is

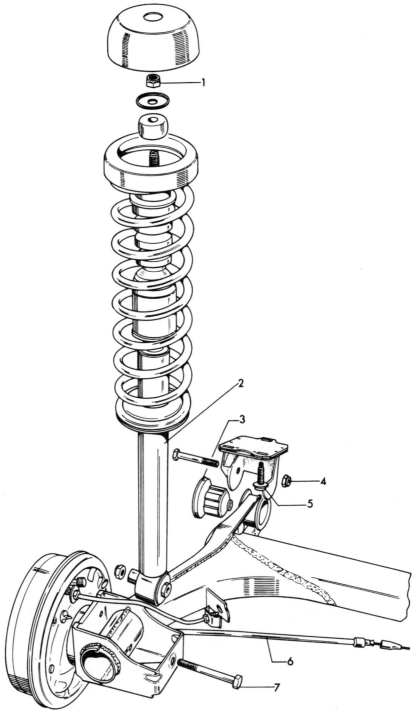

FIG 8:1   Rear suspension components

Key to Fig 8:1   1 Damper upper mounting nut   2 Coil spring and damper   3 Axle bush   4 Pivot bolt nut   5 Holder mounting bolt   6 Handbrake cable   7 Damper lower fixing bolt

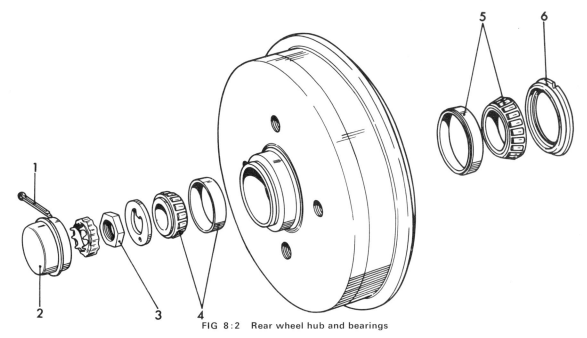

FIG 8:2   Rear wheel hub and bearings

Key to Fig 8:2   1 Splitpin   2 Grease cap   3 Hub nut   4 Outer bearing   5 Inner bearing   6 Seal

worn or damaged, renew both roller bearings and their outer races. Carefully drive the outer races from the hub using a brass drift and working evenly around the circumference to prevent jamming.

Carefully drive the new outer races into the hub up to their stops, making sure that they are kept square. Pack the new taper roller bearings with multi-purpose grease and fit them to the outer races. If the seal is not in perfect condition it should be renewed. Carefully drive the seal into place. Make certain that no trace of grease or oil remains inside the brake drum, then fit the hub and drum to the stub axle. Refit the washer and hub nut, then adjust the wheel bearings as described previously. On completion, check the rear brake adjustment as described in **Chapter 10**.

8:3 Rear axle

Removal:

Raise and safely support the rear of the car, remove the road wheels and release the handbrake. Disconnect the rear section of the exhaust pipe and lower it carefully. Wire the exhaust pipe to the body to prevent excessive strain. Refer to **FIG 8:4** and remove handbrake roller and adjusting nut. Unscrew the brake pressure governor linkage as shown in **FIG 8:5**. Refer to **FIG 8:6** and disconnect the brake hose from the brake pipe at the connector. Plug the hose and pipe to prevent loss of fluid or entry of dirt.

Use suitable jacks or stands to support the axle, then remove the nuts from the bolts 7 securing the damper

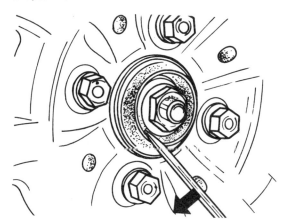

FIG 8:3   Checking wheel bearing adjustment

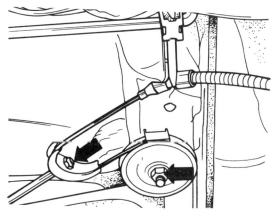

FIG 8:4   Removing handbrake roller and adjusting nut

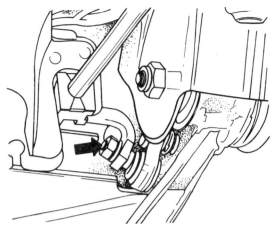

FIG 8:5 Unscrewing brake pressure governor linkage

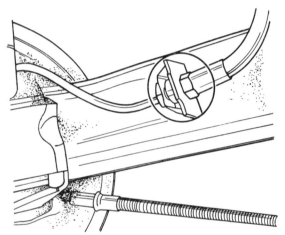

FIG 8:6 Brake pipe connection

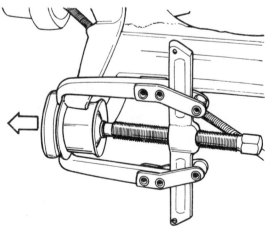

FIG 8:7 Axle bearing removal

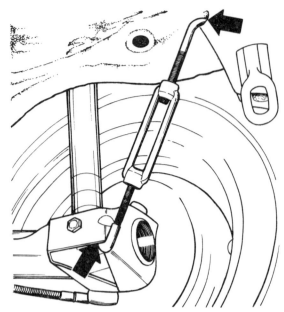

FIG 8:8 Holding axle with the special tool

lower ends (see **FIG 8:1**). Access to these nuts is through the hole in the rear of the axle unit. Unscrew nuts 4 on each side, then remove the pivot bolts and detach the rear axle assembly from the car. **Never loosen bolts 5 during axle removal as this would dictate the resetting of the holder plates which is a specialist job.**

Refitting:

This is a reversal of the removal procedure using new self-locking nuts. Tighten nut 4 to 57Nm (41lb ft) and the nut for bolt 7 to 45Nm (32.5lb ft). On completion, bleed the brakes and adjust the handbrake mechanism as described in **Chapter 10**.

Axle bearing renewal:

The rear axle rubber bearings can be renewed with the axle installed. Raise and safely support the rear of the car. Remove nuts 4 on each side and remove the pivot bolts (see **FIG 8:1**). Pull down on the axle until the bushes are clear of the holders. Use a suitable puller to remove the bushes from the axle bores as shown in **FIG 8:7**. Install the new bushes in the reverse order, then refit the pivot bolts with new nuts, tightening to 45Nm (32.5lb ft).

8:4 Suspension struts
Removal:

Raise and safely support the rear of the car then remove the road wheel. Fit tool 3004 as shown in **FIG 8:8** or use a jack to support the rear axle. From inside the car, take off the cover and remove the nut shown at 1 in **FIG 8:1**, holding the central rod with a screwdriver while doing so. Remove the nut from bolt 7 (see **FIG 8 : 1**) then remove the bolt to release the lower end of the damper.

Disconnect the brake hose from the brake pipe at the connector shown in **FIG 8 : 6**. Plug the pipe and hose to prevent loss of fluid or entry of dirt. Turn tool 3004 or carefully lower the jack to lower the axle until the suspension struts and coil spring assembly can be removed from the car. Take care not to damage the handbrake cable.

Refitting:

This is a reversal of the removal procedure. Use a new self-locking nut to secure the upper end of the suspension strut, tightened to 20Nm (14.5lb ft). On completion, bleed the brakes as described in **Chapter 10**.

8 : 5 Rear wheel geometry

Whenever suspension components have been dismantled or at any time when uneven tyre wear has been noted, the rear suspension setting angles should be checked. The correct setting angles are given in **Technical Data** in the **Appendix**. The checking of rear suspension angles should be carried out at a service station having special optical measuring equipment. Note that rear wheel camber and toe-in settings are not adjustable, so if found to be incorrect a check should be made on rear suspension components for damage or distortion.

8 : 6 Fault diagnosis

(a) Wheel wobble

1 Worn hub bearings
2 Worn axle bushes
3 Uneven tyre wear
4 Loose wheel fixings
5 Incorrect wheel geometry

(b) Bottoming of suspension

1 Broken or weak spring
2 Ineffective dampers
3 Car overloaded.

(c) Rattles

1 Worn bushes
2 Damper attachments loose

(d) Excessive tyre wear

1 Check 2 and 5 in (a)

NOTES

CHAPTER 9

THE STEERING GEAR

9:1 Description

Rack and pinion steering is employed. The pinion shaft is turned by the lower end of the steering column shaft and moves the rack to the left or right, transmitting the steering motion to the front wheels by means of the tie rods and the arms on the steering knuckles. The rack and pinion are held in mesh by a spring and plate, the spring pressure being adjustable to compensate for wear. The steering gear housing is held to the bodywork by means of clamps. The tie rod ends are connected to the steering knuckle arms by means of ball joint assemblies, a threaded sleeve being provided to allow for front wheel toe-in adjustment.

Apart from regular checks on the general condition of the steering gear components, no routine maintenance is necessary as all components are factory lubricated and sealed for life. The rubber boots on steering gear and ball joints should be examined for splits, holes or other damage and renewed if any fault is found. At the same time, check the ball joints for excessive play. If evidence of looseness is found or if a ball joint rubber boot is damaged, the ball joint in question must be renewed. A damaged rubber boot will allow the entry of dirt and grit which will cause rapid wear.

9:2 Steering gear adjustment

If the steering gear has excessive free play, or is abnormally stiff in operation, first check for worn ball joints or a binding steering linkage, before carrying out steering gear adjustment.

Raise the front of the car and safely support on floor stands. Set the steering in the straightahead position. **FIG 9:1** shows the self-locking adjusting screw on the steering gear. The screw must be turned anti-clockwise to reduce stiffness in the steering gear, or turned clockwise to take up free play or looseness. Turn the screw approximately 20° at a time and check that the steering wheel can be turned from lock to lock with no sign of binding after each adjustment. Carefully road test the car and check that the steering returns unassisted to the straightahead position after making a turn. If any stiffness in operation is noticed, the adjusting screw must be loosened a little to free the steering gear.

9:3 Steering column

Removal:

Turn the steering wheel until the road wheels are in the straightahead position. Disconnect the battery. Remove

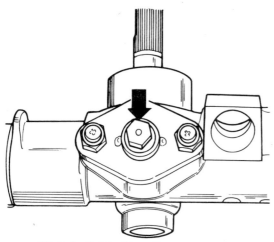

FIG 9:1   Self-locking adjustment screw

the lower instrument panel trim, then unscrew the lower column clamp as shown in **FIG 9:3**. Lever the flanged tube from the steering pinion as shown in **FIG 9:4**.

Pull off the horn bar by hand, then disconnect the wiring connectors (see **FIG 9:5**). Remove the fixing nut, then pull the steering wheel from the splined shaft. Loosen the clamping screw arrowed in **FIG 9:6**, then remove the combination switch and pull off both connector plugs. Remove the instrument panel trim.

Unscrew the steering lock assembly as shown in **FIG 9:7**, then disconnect the plug connector at the ignition switch.

Refitting:

This is a reversal of the removal procedure, noting the following points:

Adjust the distance between steering wheel and combination switch until dimension **A** in **FIG 9:8** is 2 to 3mm. Fit a new self-locking nut to the lower clamp bolt, tighten to 25Nm (18lb ft) and check that the adjustment has not altered. Make sure that the steering wheel is refitted with the spokes horizontal when the road wheels are straightahead, tightening the fixing nut to 30Nm (21.5lb ft).

Steering/ignition lock cylinder:

Removal:

Remove the steering column trim then mark the switch housing as shown in **FIG 9:9** and drill a 3mm hole through the housing. Remove the ignition key and press the retaining spring in with a punch or screwdriver and pull the cylinder out by hand. Note that the cylinder can only be removed and installed with the key taken out of the lock. To refit, push the cylinder into place until the retaining spring engages.

9:4 Steering gear removal and refitting

Tie rod removal:

Refer to **FIG 9:10**. Remove the ball joint nut from the outer end of the tie rod to be removed, then free the ball

joint from the steering arm using a suitable puller as shown in **FIG 9:11**. Remove the nut and bolt securing the inner end of the tie rod to the steering gear, then remove the tie rod.

If one of the joints is worn or damaged on the longer tie rod, the entire one-piece assembly must be renewed. The joints on the shorter tie rod can be removed and replaced individually. If one of these joints is to be removed, slacken the locknut and unscrew the joint, counting the number of turns taken to do so. When the joint is fitted to the tie rod, screw it on by the same number of turns as counted previously. Tighten the locknut gently to temporarily secure the ball joint in this position, until front wheel alignment is corrected when the work is complete.

Refitting:

This is a reversal of the removal procedure. Tighten nuts 1 to 37Nm (27lb ft), nuts 2 to 40Nm (29lb ft) and nuts 9 to 23Nm (16.5lb ft). On completion, check front wheel alignment as described in **Section 9:5**.

Steering gear removal:

On some models, access to the steering gear must be improved by removing the windscreen washer container from the engine compartment. From inside the car, remove the lefthand shelf. Refer to **Chapter 5** and disconnect the clutch cable from the clutch release lever and the fitting on the transmission.

Refer to **FIG 9:3** and slacken lower column clamp (lefthand arrow) and disconnect clutch cable from pedal (righthand arrow). Lever the flanged tube from the steering pinion as shown in **FIG 9:4**. Unscrew the nuts shown at 9 in **FIG 9:10**, then remove the bolts and detach the tie rods at their inner ends. Remove nuts 7 and detach the steering gear clamps. Drive out the clutch cable sleeve with a soft-faced hammer.

Check the steering gear for wear or damage. Renew the rubber boot if it is damaged or perished. If the steering gear is excessively tight or loose in operation and this cannot be cured by correct adjustment as described in **Section 9:2**, internal wear or damage is indicated and the steering gear assembly should be renewed.

Refitting:

This is a reversal of the removal procedure. Always use a new self-locking nut at the column lower clamp, tightened to 25Nm (18lb ft). Make sure that the steering wheel spokes are horizontal and the front wheels in the straightahead position before tightening the clamp. Tighten nuts 7 and 9 to 23Nm (16.5lb ft). If nut 8 has been slackened it should be retightened to 40Nm (29lb ft). On completion, check front wheel alignment as described in **Section 9:5** and clutch adjustment as described in **Chapter 5**.

9:5   Front wheel alignment

When correctly adjusted, the front wheels will toe-in by − 0° 10' to + 0° 9' (− 2.1 to + 1.9mm). Measurement must be carried out with the car at kerb weight, which is unloaded but with spare wheel and a full fuel tank and

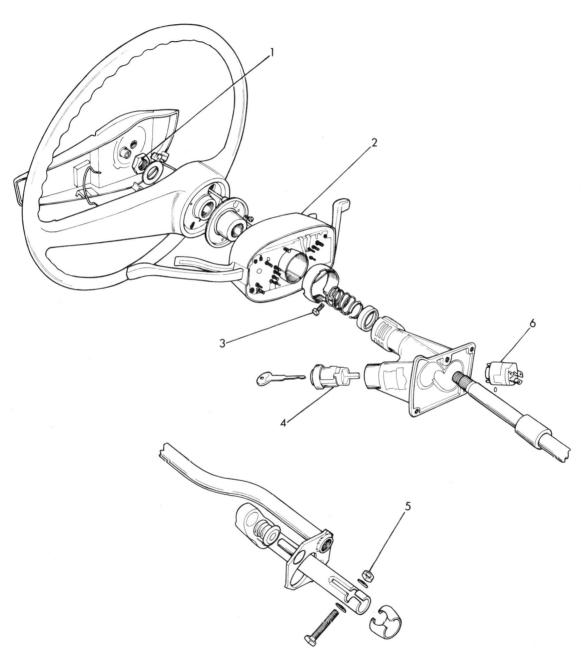

FIG 9:2 Steering column components

Key to Fig 9:2   1 Steering wheel nut   2 Combination switch   3 Clamp screw   4 Lock cylinder   5 Clamp nut
6 Ignition/starter switch

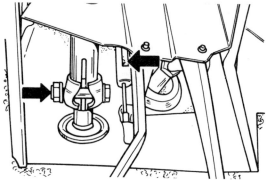

FIG 9:3 Lower column clamp (left) and clutch cable connection (right)

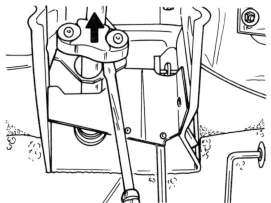

FIG 9:4 Flanged tube removal

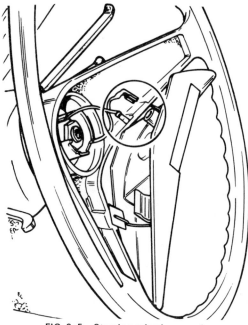

FIG 9:5 Steering wheel removal

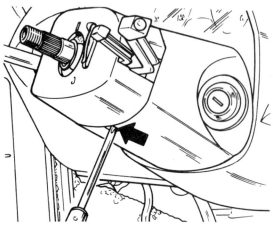

FIG 9:6 Combination switch removal

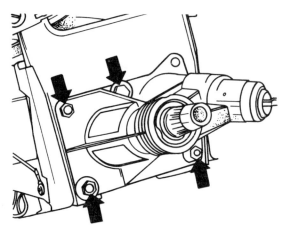

FIG 9:7 Steering lock removal

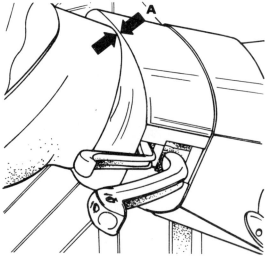

FIG 9:8 Adjusting clearance between steering wheel and combination switch

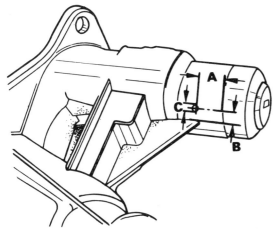

FIG 9:9 Steering/ignition lock cylinder removal

Key to Fig 9:9   A = 12.5mm   B = 6.5mm   C = 3mm

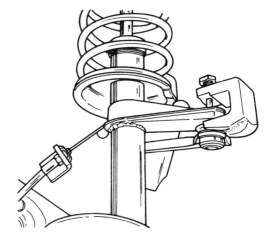

FIG 9:11   Detaching tie rod ball joint

the tyres inflated to the recommended pressures. Before measurements are taken, the car should be bounced at front and rear to bottom the springs. This procedure settles the suspension correctly. Set the steering to the straightahead position and check the wheel alignment with an approved track setting gauge. Push the car forward until the wheels have turned through 180° and recheck.

If adjustment is required, refer to **FIG 9:10** and loosen the clamp nuts 2 at each end of the adjustable tie rod. Turn the tie rod itself, for which purpose a flat is provided, until the alignment is correct. Tighten clamp bolts 2 to 40Nm (29lb ft), then recheck the setting. If the correct measuring equipment is not available, have the work carried out at a service station.

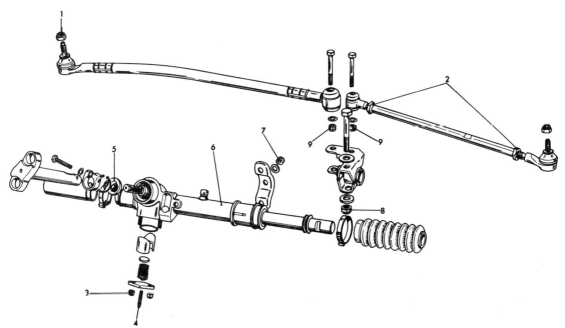

FIG 9:10   Steering gear components

Key to Fig 9:10   1 Ball joint nut   2 Tie rod locknuts   3 Adjuster plate nut   4 Self-locking adjustment screw   5 Clamp nut   6 Steering gear assembly   7 Steering gear clamp nut   8 Tie rod connector clamp nut   9 Tie rod inner joint nuts

9:6 Fault diagnosis

(a) Wheel wobble

1 Unbalanced wheels and tyres
2 Slack steering connections
3 Incorrect steering geometry
4 Excessive play in steering gear
5 Faulty suspension
6 Worn hub bearings

(b) Heavy steering

1 Check 3 in (a)
2 Very low tyre pressures
3 Neglected lubrication
4 Wheel alignment incorrect

5 Steering gear adjustment too tight
6 Steering column shaft bent
7 Tight bearings

(c) Wander

1 Check 2, 3 and 4 in (a)
2 Uneven tyre pressures
3 Uneven tyre wear
4 Ineffective dampers

(d) Lost motion

1 Loose steering wheel
2 Worn steering gear assembly
3 Worn ball joints
4 Worn steering knuckles
5 Worn suspension ball joints

CHAPTER 10

THE BRAKING SYSTEM

10:1 Description

The braking system follows conventional practice, with hydraulically operated disc brakes on the front wheels, drum brakes on the rear wheels and a cable-operated handbrake linkage which operates on the rear brakes only.

The brakes on all four wheels are operated hydraulically, pressure on the brake fluid being generated in the master cylinder which is connected by a pushrod to the brake pedal.

In order to ensure properly balanced braking under all load conditions and to prevent rear wheel locking under heavy braking, a pressure governor valve is fitted into the circuit. This valve is mechanically operated through a linkage connected to the rear suspension, so that under light rear end loads pressure to the rear brake units is reduced, while pressure is increased when the rear of the car is more heavily loaded.

10:2 Routine maintenance

Regularly check the level of fluid in the master cylinder reservoir and replenish if necessary. Wipe dirt from around the cap before removing it and check that the vent hole in the cap is unobstructed. The fluid level should be maintained at the MAX mark on the reservoir. If frequent topping up is required, the system should be checked for leaks, but it should be noted that with disc brake systems the fluid level will drop gradually over a period of time due to the movement of caliper pistons compensating for friction pad wear. The recommended fluid is one conforming to US Standard FMVSS 116 DOT 3, such as genuine Volkswagen Brake Fluid. **Never use anything but the recommended fluid.**

At the intervals recommended in the service booklet, the brake fluid in the system should be completely changed. This can be carried out by opening a bleed screw and pumping out the old brake fluid by operating the brake pedal. The system should then be filled with fresh brake fluid of the correct type and the brakes bled as described in **Section 10:6**. Alternatively, the work can be carried out very quickly by pressure-bleeding at a service station.

Checking brake pads and linings:

Regularly check the thickness of friction lining material on the front brake pads and the rear brake shoes. To

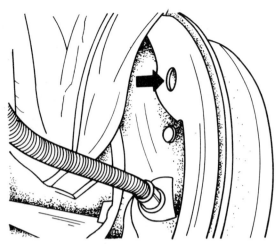

FIG 10:1   Rear brake lining inspection hole

check front brake pad thickness, raise the front of the car and remove the road wheels. Look into the front of the caliper recess and examine the friction pads. If any pad has worn to a thickness of 2mm (0.08in) or if any pad is cracked or oily, all four friction pads must be renewed.

To check the lining thickness on rear brakes, raise and safely support the rear of the car and remove the road wheels. Remove the blanking plug and inspect the lining thickness through the hole provided in the brake backplate (see **FIG 10:1**). If any lining has worn to the point where the total thickness of lining and shoe is 5.0mm (0.20in) for riveted linings or 3.5mm (0.14in) for bonded linings, or if any lining is damaged or oily, all four rear brake linings should be renewed.

Brake adjustment:

Whenever brake pedal travel becomes excessive, the rear brakes should be adjusted to move the brake shoes closer to the drums. Always check that the linings are not worn to the limit before carrying out the adjustment procedure described in **Section 10:3**.

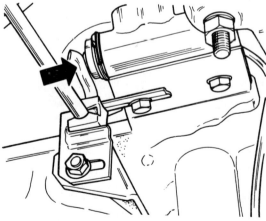

FIG 10:2   Releasing rear circuit fluid pressure

The front disc brakes are self-adjusting, due to the action of the operating pistons in the calipers. These pistons are returned to the rest position after each brake operation by the piston seals, the seals being slightly stretched during brake operation. As the friction pads wear, the piston stroke is increased and the piston will travel further than before and move through the stretched seal a little, the seal returning the piston to a new position nearer the pads when the brakes are released. In this manner the piston stroke remains constant regardless of the thickness of friction pad linings.

Adjustment of the rear brake shoes will normally maintain the handbrake adjustment correctly, but if the handbrake cable has stretched in service, or if the mechanism has been reassembled after overhaul, the handbrake should be adjusted as described in **Section 10:8**.

10:3 Drum brakes

Adjustment:

Raise the rear of the car and support safely on floor stands. Chock the front wheels against rotation and fully release the handbrake.

It is necessary to fully release fluid pressure in the rear brake circuit otherwise the righthand rear brake will be held partly on, making accurate adjustment impossible. To do this, press the lever on the brake pressure governor once, in the direction of the arrow in **FIG 10:2**. This will eliminate any remaining fluid pressure.

Remove the blanking plugs at the rear of each brake backplate for access to the adjusters, which are arrowed in **FIG 10:3**. Insert a suitable screwdriver through the access hole to turn the adjuster wheel. Spin the road wheel and turn the adjuster until the shoes lock the wheel against rotation, then slacken off until the wheel is just free to turn. Repeat the adjustment procedure on the opposite rear wheel, then operate the footbrake and handbrake several times. Fully release the handbrake, release the rear system fluid pressure as previously described, then recheck that both rear wheels can spin freely with no sign of binding. If a brake can be felt to bind when the wheel is turned slowly by hand, slacken off the appropriate adjuster a little more until the wheel is quite free to turn.

Removing brake shoes:

Raise and safely support the rear of the car on floor stands. Chock the front wheels against rotation and fully release the handbrake. Remove the brake drum and wheel hub assembly as described in **Chapter 8, Section 8:2**. Safely store the loose wheel bearing components to avoid contamination by dirt or grit, and avoid getting grease on to the inside of the brake drum or on to the brake linings themselves.

Refer to **FIG 10:4**. Carefully lever off springs **a**, then release spring **b**. Use a suitable pair of pliers to disconnect springs **c**. Remove the brake shoes and disconnect the handbrake cable.

Servicing:

Clean all grease, dirt and dust from the brake backplate and drum. Inspect the inside surface of the drum against

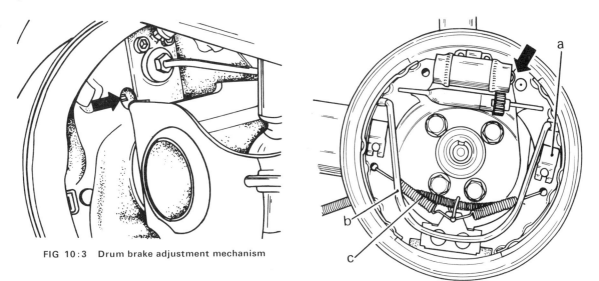

FIG 10:3   Drum brake adjustment mechanism

FIG 10:4   Brake shoe removal

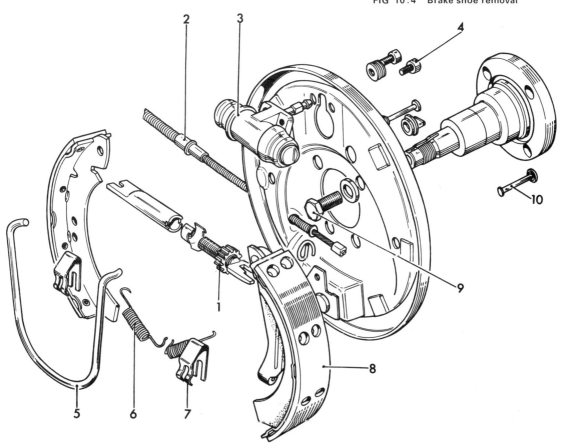

FIG 10:5   Rear brake components

Key to Fig 10:5   1 Adjustment mechanism   2 Handbrake cable   3 Wheel cylinder   4 Cylinder attachment screws
5 Main return spring   6 Secondary return spring   7 Retaining clip   8 Brake shoe   9 Backplate retaining bolt   10 Retaining
pin

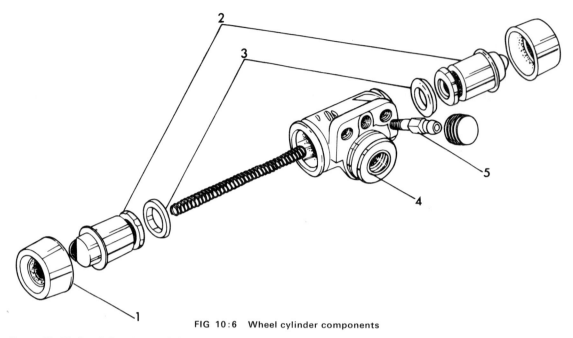

FIG 10:6 Wheel cylinder components

Key to Fig 10:6   1 Dust boot   2 Pistons   3 Sealing cups   4 Wheel cylinder   5 Bleed screw

which the brake shoes operate. Slight scoring is unimportant, but heavy scoring will dictate resurfacing at a service station or, if this treatment is not successful, renewal of the drum. If any brake fluid is leaking from the wheel cylinder, service the unit as described later.

It is not recommended that owners attempt to reline brake shoes themselves. It is important that the linings are properly bedded to the shoes and ground for concentricity with the brake drum. For this reason it is best to obtain sets of replacement shoes on an exchange basis, or have the shoes relined at a service station. Do not allow grease, oil or brake fluid to contaminate brake linings. If the linings are contaminated in any way they must be renewed, as they cannot be successfully cleaned.

Refitting:

Make sure that the brake shoe webs are correctly fitted to the wheel cylinder pistons as shown by the arrow in **FIG 10:4**. Correctly install the adjuster mechanism between the shoes and the handbrake cable to the rear shoe as shown in **FIG 10:5**. On completion, refit the hub and drum and adjust the wheel bearing as described in **Chapter 8, Section 8:2**, then adjust the rear brakes as described previously.

Servicing a wheel cylinder:

Raise the rear of the car and remove the road wheel, brake drum and brake shoes as described previously. Disconnect the brake fluid pipe from the cylinder and plug the pipe to prevent fluid loss. Remove the mounting screws shown at 4 in **FIG 10:5**, then detach the wheel cylinder from the backplate.

Remove the rubber dust boots then remove the pistons, seals and spring as shown in **FIG 10:6**. Wash all parts thoroughly in methylated spirits or clean brake fluid of the correct type and inspect them for wear or damage. Any part which is unserviceable must be renewed. Always fit new rubber seals and dust boots.

Smear the pistons and seals with ATE Brake Cylinder Paste and reassemble them together with the spring, using the fingers only for this operation to avoid damage to the seals. Carefully fit the rubber dust boots to the wheel cylinder. Refit the wheel cylinder to the brake backplate, tightening the fixing screws to 8Nm (6lb ft). Reconnect the brake fluid pipe to the wheel cylinder. Refit the brake shoes and drum as described previously.

On completion, bleed the braking system as described in **Section 10:6** then adjust the rear brakes as described previously.

10:4 Disc brakes

Friction pad renewal:

Apply the handbrake, raise the front of the car and support safely on stands, then remove the road wheels. Siphon sufficient brake fluid from the reservoir to bring the level down to the halfway mark. If this is not done, fluid will overflow when the new pads are fitted and the pistons pressed back into position.

Drive out the pad retaining pins towards the centre of the car and remove the cross spring, as shown in **FIG 10:7**. Discard the retaining pins and cross spring, as new parts, which must always be fitted, are supplied with the new brake pads.

Pull out the inner brake pad, using tool 60-502 or similar as shown in **FIG 10:8**. Pull the caliper floating

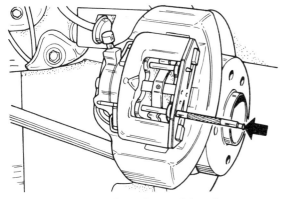

FIG 10:7   Removing retaining pins

frame outwards to release the outer brake pad tab, (see **FIG 10:9**) then remove the outer brake pad. Mark the pads for refitting in their original positions if they are not to be renewed.

Check that the new pads are of the correct type and that they are free from grease, oil and dirt. Clean dirt and rust from the caliper before fitting the pads. To enable the new pads to be fitted, push the caliper piston down into its bore to allow for the extra thickness of the pads, using tool 60-500 or other suitable means, as shown in **FIG 10:10**. Note that this operation will cause the level of brake fluid in the master cylinder reservoir to rise, this being the reason for siphoning off some of the fluid.

Use tool 60-503 or other suitable gauge to check that the cut out in the piston is at 20° to the caliper body, as shown in **FIG 10:11**. If piston position is incorrect, use pliers 60-501 or other suitable tool to rotate the piston as necessary. Take care not to damage the piston or the rubber boot

Fit the new outer brake pad, making sure that the guide tab is correctly located in the floating frame. Press the floating frame inwards, then fit the inner brake pad. Fit the new retaining pins and cross spring, tapping the pins fully home. On completion, operate the brake pedal several times to bring the pads close to the disc. If this is not done, the brakes may not function the first time that they are used. Check that the pads are free to move slightly in the caliper, this indicating that the pad retaining pins are not fouling the pads. Refit the road wheels and lower the car. Road test to check the brakes.

Removing and dismantling a caliper:

Apply the handbrake, raise the front of the car and safely support on floor stands before removing the road wheel. If the caliper is to be removed for access to other components only, remove the two caliper mounting bolts and support the caliper by wiring to the suspension so that the hose is not strained. The hose remains connected to the caliper therefore it will not be necessary to bleed the system after refitting the caliper.

If the caliper is to be dismantled, remove the brake pads as described previously, then disconnect the fluid hose from the caliper and plug the end of the hose to prevent fluid loss. Remove the two fixing bolts arrowed in **FIG 7:3**, then lift off the caliper.

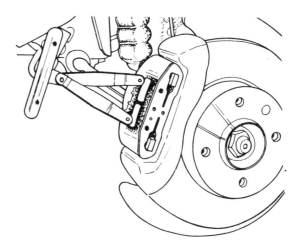

FIG 10:8   Removing inner brake pad

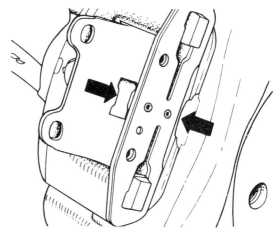

FIG 10:9   Removing outer brake pad

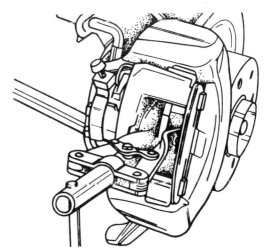

FIG 10:10   Pressing piston into the caliper bore

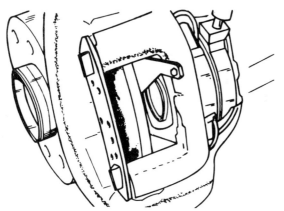

FIG 10:11   Checking position of piston cutout

FIG 10:12 shows caliper components. Clean road dirt from the outside of the caliper, using methylated spirits as a solvent if necessary. Carefully lever the holder from the assembly as shown in **FIG 10:13**. Remove the retaining rings shown at 11 in **FIG 10:12**, then remove dust boot 12.

Slide a suitable piece of wood through the floating frame and hold in position to prevent the piston from flying out of the cylinder too quickly. Eject the piston by applying an airline nozzle to the brake hose connection at the cylinder. If an airline is not available, temporarily reconnect the cylinder to the brake pipe on the vehicle, then have an assistant depress the brake pedal very slowly until the piston is pushed out far enough to be removed with the fingers. Remove the caliper cylinder with guide spring from the floating frame.

Carefully remove the seal shown at 14 in **FIG 10:12**, avoiding the use of sharp tools which would damage the

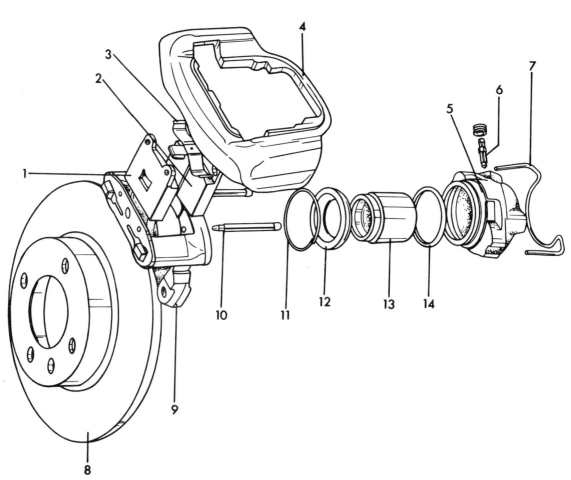

FIG 10:12   Caliper components

Key to Fig 10:12   1 Outer brake pad   2 Inner brake pad   3 Cross spring   4 Floating frame   5 Cylinder body   6 Bleed screw   7 Guide spring   8 Brake disc   9 Pad holder   10 Retaining pin   11 Retaining ring   12 Dust boot   13 Piston   14 Seal

cylinder bore. Discard the dust boot and piston seal, then wash the remaining internal parts with methylated spirits or clean approved brake fluid. **Use no other cleaner or solvent on brake components.** Inspect all parts for wear or damage and the piston and cylinder bore for scoring or pitting. Renew any parts found worn, damaged or corroded, making sure that the correct replacement part is obtained and fitted.

Reassembly and refitting:

Use new piston seal and dust boot. Apply a thin coat of ATE Brake Cylinder Paste to cylinder, piston, seal and inside of the dust boot during assembly. Observe absolute cleanliness to prevent the entry of dirt or any trace of oil or grease. Use the fingers only to fit the piston seal to avoid damage, making sure that it is properly seated in the cylinder groove as shown in **FIG 10:14**.

Fit the brake cylinder into the floating frame as shown in **FIG 10:15**, noting that the bent leg of the guide spring rests on the disc aperture. Make sure that the piston and dust boot are correctly fitted and press the piston to the bottom of its bore. Fit the holder to the guide spring as shown in **FIG 10:16** and slide it on to the floating frame. The holder is provided with grooves and is guided by ribs on the floating frame.

Refit the brake pads as described previously then install the caliper and tighten the mounting bolts to 57Nm (41lb ft). Connect the fluid hose to the caliper then bleed the brakes as described in **Section 10:6**.

Brake disc removal:

Remove the brake caliper and wire it to the suspension as described previously. Remove the single locating screw and withdraw the brake disc from the wheel hub. Refitting is a reversal of the removal procedure. Tighten the locating screw to 5Nm (3.5lb ft).

10:5 The master cylinder

Removal:

The brake pedal and master cylinder assembly are shown in **FIG 10:17**. Detach the wiring connectors from the switch on the master cylinder body. Disconnect the brake fluid pipes from the cylinder, using plugs to prevent loss of fluid and the entry of dirt. Hold a piece of rag beneath the master cylinder to catch any fluid which escapes, as brake fluid can damage paintwork. Remove the two mounting nuts and lift the master cylinder from the vehicle. Empty the contents of the fluid reservoir into a waste container.

Servicing:

Use a small screwdriver to lever out the retaining circlip as shown in **FIG 10:18**. Dismantle the internal components into the order shown in **FIG 10:19** and discard the rubber cups. Wash the remaining parts in methylated spirits or approved brake fluid. **Use no other cleaner or solvent on brake hydraulic system components.** Inspect the piston and cylinder bore for score marks and inspect all parts for wear or damage. Renew any faulty parts. Always use new rubber cups.

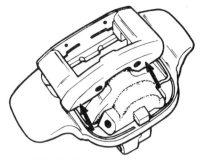

FIG 10:13   Removing holder

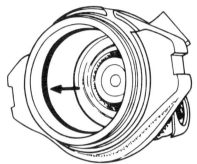

FIG 10:14   Fitting piston seal

FIG 10:15   Fitting cylinder to floating frame

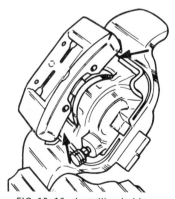

FIG 10:16   Installing holder

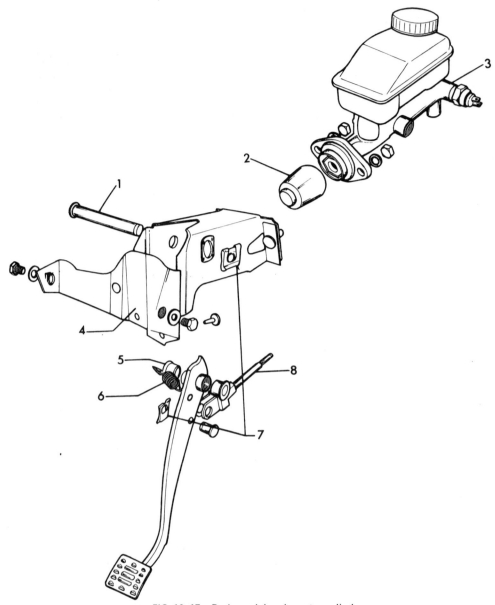

FIG 10:17   Brake pedal and master cylinder

Key to Fig 10:17   1 Pedal shaft   2 Dust boot   3 Master cylinder assembly   4 Mounting bracket   5 Bushes   6 Return spring   7 Lock plates   8 Master cylinder pushrod

Reassembly:

Observe absolute cleanliness to prevent the entry of dirt or any trace of oil or grease. Use the fingers only to fit the new rubber piston cups to prevent damage. Apply a thin coat of ATE Brake Cylinder Paste to all internal parts during assembly. Reassemble in the reverse order of dismantling, taking care that the separating cup is correctly fitted, using a conical tool as shown in **FIG**

10:20. Take great care not to turn back the lips of the piston cups when installing them in the cylinder bore. Make sure that the fluid feed and compensation holes in the cylinder body are clear.

Refitting:

This is a reversal of the removal procedure. On completion, fill the fluid reservoir to the correct level then bleed the brakes as described in **Section 10:6**. Check the master cylinder pushrod clearance and adjust if necessary as described next. Before road testing the car to check the operation of the brakes, apply heavy pressure to the brake pedal and hold for at least ten seconds, before examining the master cylinder for any signs of fluid leakage.

Master cylinder pushrod clearance:

Pushrod clearance is correct when there is between 2 and 4mm of freeplay at the brake pedal pad. To check free play, first make sure that the brake pedal is held firmly against its stop by the return spring shown at 6 in **FIG 10:17**, then press the pedal gently by hand and measure the distance moved by the pedal pad before resistance is felt. If free play is incorrect, slacken the locknut securing pushrod 8 (see **FIG 10:17**) to the pedal clevis, then rotate the pushrod until the correct figure is obtained. Tighten the locknut firmly and recheck the play.

10:6 Bleeding the system

This is not routine maintenance and is only necessary if air has entered the hydraulic system due to parts being dismantled, or because the level in the master cylinder supply reservoir has been allowed to drop too low. The need for bleeding is indicated by a spongy feeling at the brake pedal accompanied by poor braking performance. Each brake must be bled in turn, in the following order: Rear righthand, rear lefthand, front righthand and front lefthand. **Do not attempt to bleed the brakes with any drum or caliper removed.**

Remove the reservoir cap and top up the reservoir to the correct level with approved brake fluid. Clean dirt from around the first bleed screw and remove the rubber dust cap. Fit a length of rubber or plastic tube to the screw and lead the free end of the tube into a clean glass jar containing a small amount of approved brake fluid. The end of the tube must remain immersed in the fluid during the bleeding operation.

Unscrew the bleed screw about half a turn and have an assistant depress the brake pedal fully. With the pedal held down tighten the bleed screw. Allow the pedal to

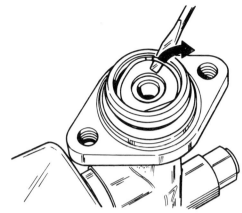

FIG 10:18   Circlip removal

return fully and wait a few seconds for the master cylinder to refill before repeating the operation. Continue operating the pedal in this manner until no air bubbles can be seen in the fluid flowing into the jar, then hold the pedal against the floor on a down stroke while the bleed valve is tightened. **Do not overtighten.**

At frequent intervals during the operation, check the level of fluid in the reservoir, topping up as needed. If the level drops too low air will enter the system and the operation will have to be restarted.

Remove the bleed tube, refit the dust cap and repeat the operation on each other brake unit in the order previously stated. Note that, if the vehicle is raised for better access to the bleed screws at the rear, it should be supported with floor stands beneath the rear suspension members or the rear wheels driven on to ramps. If the rear suspension is allowed to hang free, the governor which controls pressure supply to the rear brake circuit will operate and make it difficult or impossible to carry out the bleeding operation satisfactorily.

On completion, top up the fluid to the correct level. Discard all used fluid. Always store brake fluid in clean sealed containers to avoid air or moisture contamination.

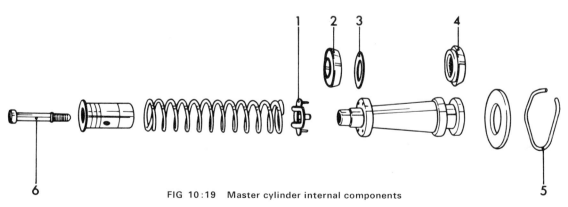

FIG 10:19   Master cylinder internal components

Key to Fig 10:19   1 Support ring   2 Primary cup   3 Spacer disc   4 Grooved cup   5 Circlip   6 Inner stop screw

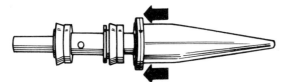

FIG 10:20 Installing separating cup with a special tool

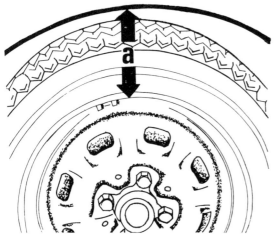

FIG 10:21 Checking rear suspension height

10:7 The brake pressure governor valve

Checking and adjusting:

This operation can only be carried out if a pair of the special tools shown in **Chapter 8**, **FIG 8:8** and appropriate brake fluid pressure gauge equipment are available. If not, the work must be left to a service station.

The tyres must be at the recommended pressures and the car must be at kerb weight, which in this context is with an empty luggage compartment, full fuel tank and a driver weighing 75kg (165lb). Under these conditions, carefully measure dimension **a** between the rear wheel rim and the top of the wheel arch as shown in **FIG 10:21**.

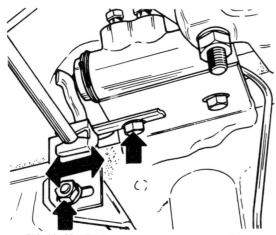

FIG 10:22 Brake pressure governor mountings

Rear axle support tools 3004 must be fitted on each side of the car as shown in **Chapter 8**, **FIG 8:8** and tightened so that, when the rear of the car is raised and safely supported, dimension **a** is exactly as previously measured with the car weight resting on the wheels.

With the suspension correctly set as just described, connect the first pressure gauge in place of the left front brake caliper bleed screw and the second pressure gauge in place of the right rear brake bleed screw. Have an assistant depress the brake pedal until pressure measured on the front gauge is 50 bar (711.01lb/sq in). With this pressure held, pressure measurement at the rear pressure gauge should be 27 to 31 bar (383 to 440lb/sq in). Now increase brake pedal pressure until front gauge reads 100 bar (1422lb/sq in). With this pressure held, pressure at the rear gauge should be 50 to 54 bar (711 to 771lb/sq in).

If rear brake fluid pressure is incorrect, slacken the governor fixings arrowed in **FIG 10:22**, move the governor assembly on the slotted mountings to adjust, then retighten the fixings. When moving the governor assembly, release pressure on governor linkage if rear brake fluid pressure is too high, or increase pressure on governor linkage if pressure is too low. **Do not make adjustments with the brake pedal depressed.** The correct sequence is to read the pressure, release the brake pedal, carry out governor adjustments, depress the brake pedal again then take the modified pressure readings. When the adjustment is correct, finally tighten the governor fixings to 21Nm (15lb ft).

On completion, remove the pressure gauges and bleed the braking system as described in **Section 10:6**.

10:8 The handbrake

Lubrication:

FIG 10:23 shows the handbrake lever components and front cable connection details. The rear cable connections are shown in **FIGS 10:5** and **10:24**. Whenever handbrake mechanism servicing or adjustment is carried out, the pivot points at the handbrake lever and at the rear cable pulley wheel should be lightly lubricated. Apply a thin smear of grease to the rear cable where it passes through the equaliser at the cable adjustment point.

Handbrake cable adjustment:

The brake shoe adjustment described in **Section 10:3** will usually take up any slack in the handbrake mechanism. If the mechanism is still slack, due to stretched cables or because the cables have been refitted after servicing, adjust the cable as follows:

Check that brake shoe adjustment is correct as described in **Section 10:3**. Raise the rear of the car and safely support on floor stands. Chock the front wheels against rotation. Fully release the handbrake, then pull the handbrake lever up by two notches on the ratchet. Now tighten the adjusting nut shown in **FIG 10:24** until the rear wheels can only just be turned by heavy hand pressure. Now release the handbrake lever fully and check that both rear wheels are free to turn with no sign of binding. If not, slacken the adjuster nut a little to correct. Operate the handbrake and footbrake several

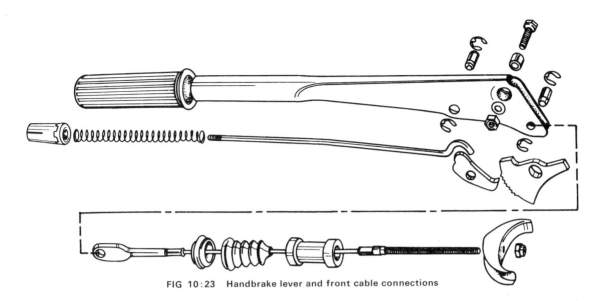

FIG 10:23   Handbrake lever and front cable connections

times, then recheck the adjustment. The adjustment nut is of the self-locking type and should be fairly stiff to turn with a spanner. If the nut is loose it should be renewed, otherwise it may loosen in service.

10:9 Fault diagnosis

(a) Spongy pedal

1 Leak in the system
2 Worn master cylinder
3 Leaking wheel or caliper cylinders
4 Air in the fluid system
5 Gaps between shoes and undersides of linings

(b) Excessive pedal movement

1 Check 1 and 4 in (a)
2 Excessive lining or pad wear
3 Very low fluid level in supply reservoir
4 Excessive brake pedal free play
5 Rear brakes require adjustment

(c) Brakes grab or pull to one side

1 Distorted discs or drums
2 Wet or oily pads or linings
3 Loose backplate or caliper
4 Disc or hub loose
5 Worn suspension or steering connections
6 Mixed linings of different grades
7 Uneven tyre pressures
8 Broken shoe return springs
9 Seized handbrake cable
10 Seized wheel cylinder or caliper piston

(d) Brakes partly or fully locked on

1 Swollen pads or linings
2 Damaged brake pipes preventing fluid return
3 Master cylinder compensating hole blocked
4 Brake pedal return spring broken
5 Master cylinder piston seized

6 Dirt in the fluid system
7 Damaged or faulty governor mechanism
8 Seized wheel cylinder or caliper piston

(e) Brake failure

1 Empty fluid reservoir
2 Broken hydraulic pipeline
3 Ruptured master cylinder seal
4 Ruptured wheel cylinder or caliper seal

(f) Reservoir empties too quickly

1 Leaks in pipelines
2 Deteriorated cylinder seals

(g) Pedal yields under continuous pressure

1 Faulty master cylinder seals
2 Faulty wheel cylinder or caliper seals

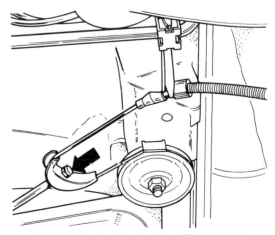

FIG 10:24   Handbrake cable adjustment nut

NOTES

CHAPTER 11

THE ELECTRICAL SYSTEM

11 :1 Description

All models covered by this manual have 12-volt electrical systems in which the negative terminal of the battery is earthed to the car bodywork.

There are wiring diagrams in **Technical Data** at the end of this manual which will enable those with electrical experience to trace and correct faults.

Instructions for servicing the items of electrical equipment are given in this chapter, but it must be pointed out that it is not sensible to try to repair units which are seriously defective, electrically or mechanically. Such faulty equipment should be replaced by new or reconditioned units which can be obtained on an exchange basis.

11 :2 The battery

To maintain the performance of the battery, it is essential to carry out the following operations, particularly in winter when heavy current demands must be met.

Keep the top and surrounding parts of the battery dry and clean, as dampness can cause current leakage. Clean off corrosion from the metal parts of the battery mounting with diluted ammonia and coat them with anti-sulphuric paint. Clean the terminal posts and smear them with petroleum jelly, tightening the terminal clamps securely. High electrical resistance due to corrosion at the battery terminals can be responsible for a lack of sufficient current to operate the starter motor.

Regularly remove the screw caps from the battery and check the electrolyte level in each cell, topping up with distilled water if necessary to the level of the marker provided in each cell.

If a battery fault is suspected, test the condition of the cells with a hydrometer. **Never add neat acid to the battery. If it is necessary to prepare new electrolyte due to loss or spillage, add sulphuric acid to distilled water. It is highly dangerous to add water to acid.** It is safest to have the battery refilled with electrolyte if it is necessary by a service station.

The indications from the hydrometer readings of the specific gravity are as follows:

For climates below 27°C or 80°F:	Specific gravity
Cell fully charged	1.270 to 1.290
Cell half discharged	1.190 to 1.210
Cell discharged	1.110 to 1.130

For climates above 27°C or 80°F:	
Cell fully charged	1.210 to 1.230
Cell half discharged	1.130 to 1.150
Cell discharged	1.050 to 1.070

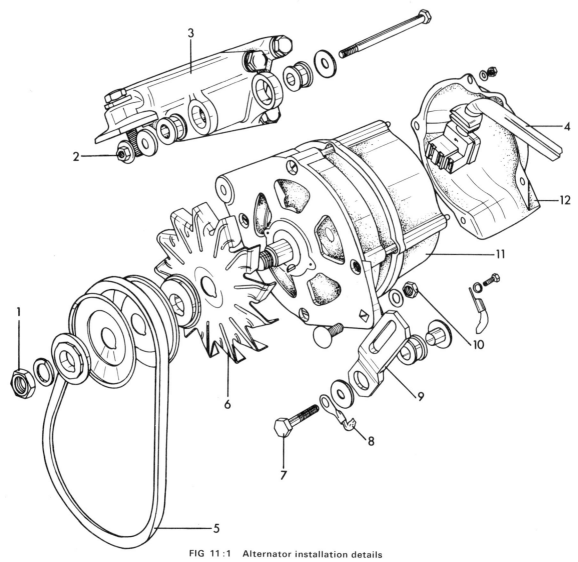

FIG 11 :1   Alternator installation details

Key to Fig 11 :1   1 Pulley nut   2 Upper mounting nut   3 Mounting   4 Wiring connector   5 Drive belt   6 Cooling fan
7 Lower mounting screw   8 Earth connection   9 Slotted plate   10 Adjustment nut   11 Alternator unit   12 Rear cover

These figures assume an electrolyte temperature of 60°F or 16°C. If the temperature of the electrolyte exceeds this, add 0.002 to the readings for each 5°F or 3°C rise. Subtract 0.002 for any corresponding drop below 60°F or 16°C.

If the battery is in a low state of charge, take the car for a long daylight run or put the battery on a charger at 5 amps, with the vents removed, until it gases freely. Do not use a naked light near the battery as the gas is inflammable. If the battery is to stand unused for long periods, give a refreshing charge every month. It will be ruined if it is left uncharged.

11 :3 The alternator

The alternator provides current for the various items of electrical equipment and to charge the battery, the unit operating at all engine speeds. The current produced is alternate, this being rectified to direct current supply by diodes mounted in the alternator casing. Alternator drive is by belt from the crankshaft pulley. Very little maintenance is needed, apart from the occasional check on belt tension as described in this section, and on the condition and tightness of the wiring connections.

The alternator must never be run with the battery disconnected, nor must the battery cables be reversed at any time. Test connections must be carefully made and the battery and alternator must be completely disconnected before any electric welding is carried out on any part of the car. The engine must never be started with a battery charger still connected to the battery. These warnings must be observed, otherwise extensive damage to the alternator components, particularly the diodes, will result.

The alternator is designed and constructed to give many years of trouble-free service. If, however, a fault should develop in the unit, it should be checked and serviced by a fully equipped service station or a reconditioned unit obtained and fitted. However, before suspecting a serious internal fault, inspect and if necessary renew the brushes as described later in this section. Alternator installation details are shown in **FIG 11:1**.

Alternator testing:

A simple check on alternator charging can be carried out after dark by switching on the headlamps and starting the engine. If the alternator is charging, the headlamps will brighten considerably as the system voltage rises from the nominal battery voltage to the higher figure produced by the alternator.

If the alternator is not charging, check the wiring and connections in the charging circuit, then check the brush gear as described later. If these are in order, the alternator unit is at fault and must be checked and repaired by a service station.

Drive belt adjustment:

The alternator drive belt is shown at 5 in **FIG 11:1**. Belt tension is correct when the belt can be deflected by 10 to 15mm (0.4 to 0.6in) by firm thumb pressure in the centre of the run between pulleys.

To adjust belt tension, slacken the upper mounting nut 2 and the lower mounting nut 10 (see **FIG 11:1**). Move the alternator body as shown by the arrow in **FIG 11:2** until belt tension is correct, then tighten first the lower mounting nut to 20Nm (14.5lb ft) then the upper mounting nut to 22Nm (16lb ft). Recheck belt tension. If a lever is used to move the alternator when tensioning the belt, it should be applied against the alternator mounting flange only. Never lever against the alternator body.

Carbon brushes:

This work can be carried out without the need for alternator removal. Remove the oil filter as described in **Chapter 1, Section 1:9**. Remove the alternator rear cover as shown at 12 in **FIG 11:1**. Remove the two screws arrowed in **FIG 11:3**, then remove the regulator assembly complete with brush holder. Inspect the carbon brushes and renew both if either is damaged or worn below the wear limit of 5mm.

To renew brushes, unsolder the old brushes at the points arrowed in **FIG 11:4**, clean carbon dust from the brush holder, then fit the new brushes and securely solder their leads to the tags.

Alternator removal:

Disconnect the battery negative cable. Disconnect the alternator lower mounting (see **FIG 11:2**) then disconnect the upper mounting as shown in **FIG 11:5**.

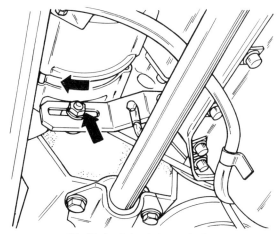

FIG 11:2   Drive belt tensioning

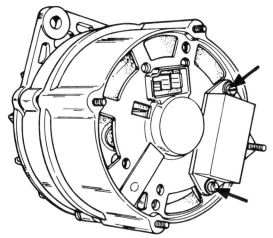

FIG 11:3   Regulator attachment screws

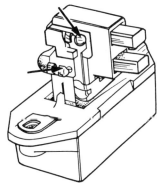

FIG 11:4   Carbon brush removal

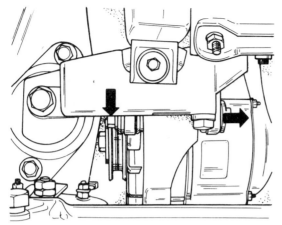

FIG 11:5   Alternator removal

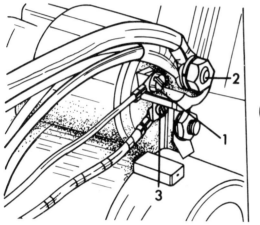

FIG 11:6   Starter motor terminals

Move the alternator towards the engine and disconnect the drive belt. Disconnect the wiring plug from the rear of the alternator. Move the alternator rearwards and lift from the engine compartment.

Refitting is a reversal of the removal procedure, adjusting the belt tension as described previously.

11:4 The starter

The starter is a brush type series wound motor equipped with an overrunning clutch and operated by a solenoid. The armature shaft is supported in metal bushes which require no routine servicing.

When the starter is operated from the switch, the engagement lever moves the pinion into mesh with the engine ring gear. When the pinion meshes with the ring gear teeth, the solenoid contact closes the circuit and the starter motor operates to turn the engine. When the engine starts, the speed of the rotating ring gear causes the pinion to overrun the clutch and armature. The pinion continues in engagement until the switch is released when the engagement lever returns it to the rest position under spring action.

Tests for a starter which does not operate:

Check that the battery is in good condition and fully charged and that its connections are clean and tight. Switch on the headlamps and operate the starter switch. Current is reaching the starter if the lights dim when the starter is operated, in which case it will be necessary to remove the starter for servicing. If the lights do not dim significantly, switch them off and operate the starter switch while listening for a clicking sound at the starter motor which will indicate that the starter solenoid is operating.

If no sound can be heard at the starter when the switch is operated, check the wiring and connections between the battery and the starter switch and between the switch and the solenoid. If the solenoid can be heard operating when the starter switch is operated, check the wiring and connections between the battery and the main starter motor terminal, taking care not to accidently earth the main battery to starter motor lead which is live at all times. If the wiring is not the cause of the trouble, the fault is internal and the starter motor must be removed and serviced.

Removing the starter:

Disconnect the earth cable from the battery. Disconnect the electrical connections from the starter motor as shown at 1, 2 and 3 in FIG 11:6. Terminal 1 was only used in earlier cars fitted with a series resistance in the ignition coil circuit. Remove the starter mounting bolts arrowed in FIG 11:7, then carefully remove the starter motor.

Refitting is a reversal of the removal procedure.

Starter dismantling:

FIG 11:8 shows the starter motor components. Free the lead of the starter motor from the lower heavy duty terminal of the solenoid by removing the nut. Remove screws 4 and detach solenoid 9, unhooking the plunger pin from the engagement lever 7.

Remove end cap 19 and detach the washers from the end of the armature shaft. Unscrew through bolts 17 and

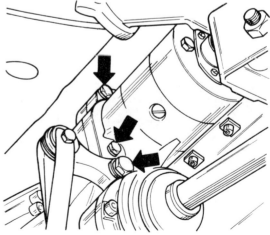

FIG 11:7   Starter motor mounting bolts

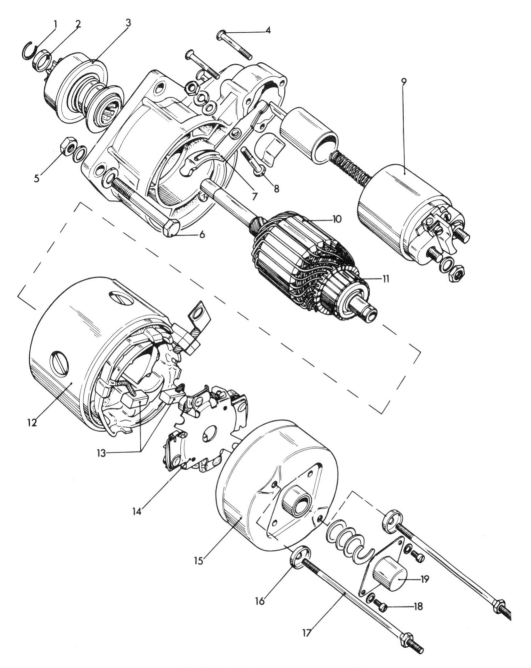

FIG 11:8 Starter motor components

Key to Fig 11:8   1 Retaining ring   2 Stop ring   3 Drive pinion assembly   4 Solenoid fixing screw   5 Nut   6 Bolt
7 Engagement lever   8 Pivot bolt   9 Solenoid   10 Armature   11 Commutator   12 Starter body   13 Brushes   14 Brush
mounting plate   15 Brush cover   16 Washer   17 Through bolt   18 Screw   19 End cap

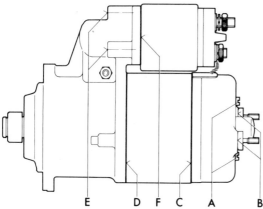

FIG 11:9 Apply sealer to the points shown when reassembling starter

detach brush cover 15. Carefully lift the springs from the ends of the brushes and withdraw the brushes from their holders. Remove brush mounting plate 14.

Remove drive pinion assembly 3 from the armature shaft by driving down the stop ring 2 with a suitable piece of tube, then removing the retaining ring 1.

Remove engagement lever pivot bolt 8, then remove armature assembly 10 and engagement lever 7.

After servicing the starter components as described later in this section, reassemble the starter in the reverse order of dismantling. Always use a new circlip shown at 1 in **FIG 11:8**. Drive the stop ring 2 onto the shaft, fit the new circlip, then use a claw puller or other suitable tool to pull the stop ring over the circlip.

During reassembly, the joint faces and screw heads shown at A, B, C, D, E and F in **FIG 11:9** must be sealed with a suitable sealing compound.

Servicing:

Brush gear:

Check the brushes for wear and renew them if they are excessively worn or contaminated. If the brushes stick in their holders, polish the sides of the brushes with a fine file and clean the brush holder with a piece of rag moistened with petrol or methylated spirits.

To renew brushes, remove the old brushes from the leads by crushing them with a pair of pliers. Clean the ends of the wires and solder them into the metal tags provided in the new brushes.

The commutator:

The commutator should have a smooth polished surface which is dark in appearance. Wiping over with a piece of cloth moistened with methylated spirits or petrol will be sufficient cleaning. Light burn marks or scores can be polished off with fine grade glasspaper (never use emerycloth as this leaves particles embedded in the copper). Deeper damage may be skimmed off in a lathe, at high speed and using a very sharp tool. A diamond tipped tool should be used for a light final cut. On completion, undercut the mica insulation between the commutator segments by 0.5 to 0.8mm. Clean away all dust from the commutator.

The armature:

Check the armature for charred insulation, loose segments or laminations and for scored laminations. Shortcircuited windings may be suspected if individual commutator segments are badly burnt. No repairs can be carried out to a defective armature and renewal is the only cure.

Field coils:

The field coils and pole pieces are held in place by special screws. To ensure correct installation and alignment, it is recommended that field coil checking and servicing be carried out at a service station.

The field coils can be checked for continuity using a test lamp and battery. A better method is to check the resistance using an ohmmeter. The resistance can also be checked using a 12-volt battery and ammeter (voltage divided by current equals resistance).

Starter drive:

Light damage to the pinion teeth can be cleaned off with a fine file or oilstone, but deeper damage necessitates renewal of the complete drive assembly.

Check that the clutch takes up drive instantaneously but slips freely in the opposite direction. Again the complete drive assembly must be renewed if the clutch is defective.

Bearings:

If the bush in the brush cover is excessively worn, it should be renewed by a service station as press equipment and very accurate mandrels are required to install the new bush.

Insulation and cleaning:

Blow away all loose dust and dirt with an air line. Use a small brush to clean out crevices. Petrol or methylated spirits may be used to help in cleaning the metal parts but the field coils, armature and drive assembly must under no circumstances be soaked with solvent.

A suitable test lamp and 12-volt battery may be used for testing purposes, though a better check would be to use a neon bulb and 110 AC volt supply. In neither case should the bulb light when connected across the insulations.

11:5 Fuses

The fuses which protect the main electrical circuits are mounted in a fuse box provided with a removable cover.

If a fuse blows, briefly check the circuit that it protects and install a new fuse. Check each circuit in turn and if the new fuse does not blow, it is likely that the old one had weakened with age. If the new fuse blows, carefully check the circuit that was live at the time and do not fit another fuse until the fault has been found and repaired. A fuse that blows intermittently will make it more difficult to correct the fault, but try shaking the wiring loom, as the fault is likely to be caused by chafed insulation making intermittent contact with engine or road vibration. **Never fit a fuse of higher rating than that specified.**

The fuse is designed to be the weak link in the circuit and if a higher rated fuse is installed the wiring may fail instead.

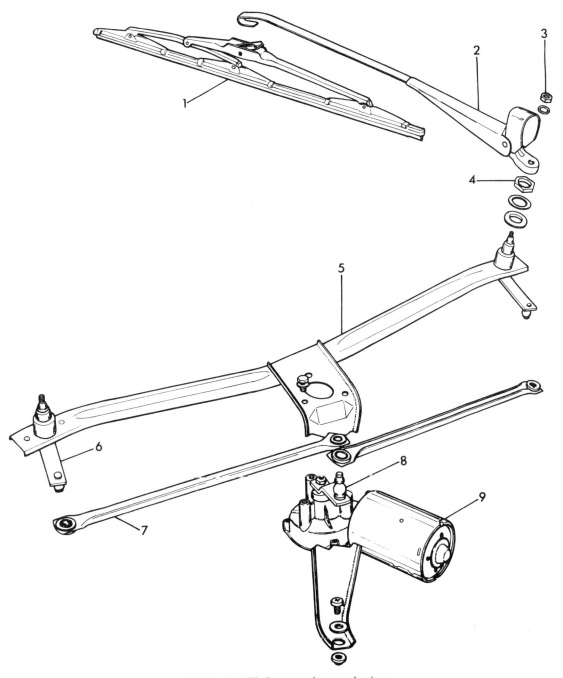

FIG 11:10 Windscreen wiper mechanism

Key to Fig 11:10   1 Wiper blade   2 Wiper arm   3 Arm attachment nut   4 Spindle base nut   5 Mounting bracket
6 Wiper bearing assembly   7 Connecting rod   8 Wiper crank   9 Wiper motor assembly

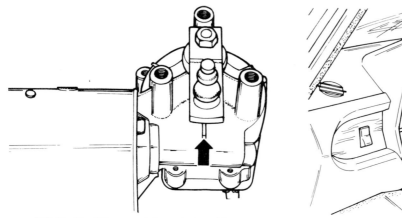

FIG 11:11   Wiper crank in parked position

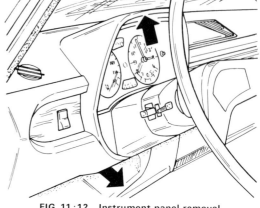

FIG 11:12   Instrument panel removal

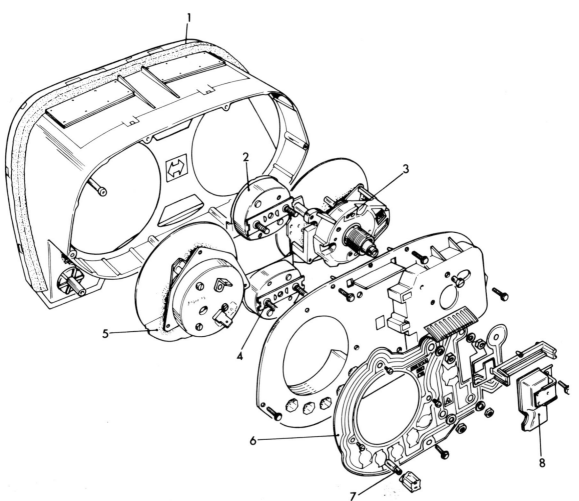

FIG 11:13   Instrument panel components

Key to Fig 11:13   1 Instrument panel housing   2 Temperature gauge   3 Speedometer   4 Fuel gauge   5 Clock (or tachometer)   6 Printed circuit board   7 Bulb   8 Voltage stabiliser

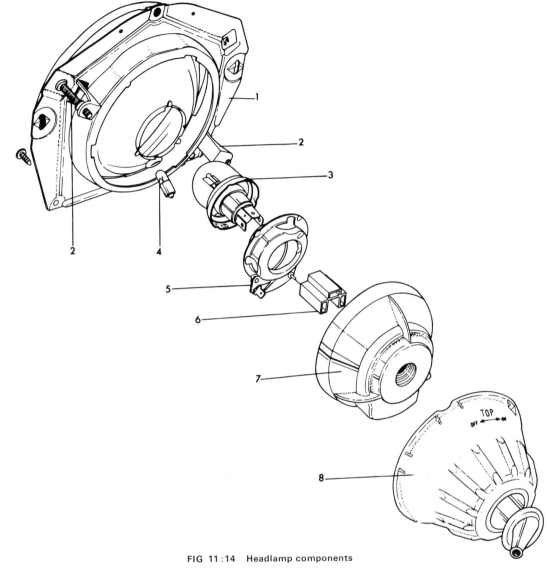

FIG 11:14   Headlamp components

Key to Fig 11:14   1 Headlamp unit   2 Adjustment screws   3 Headlamp bulb   4 Parking light bulb   5 Retaining ring
6 Connector   7 Rubber cover   8 Cap

11:6 Windscreen wiper

Windscreen wiper motors are electro-mechanical units which drive the wiper arms through linkage systems.

If wiper operation is sluggish, check the linkage for binding. If the motor is inoperative, check the fuse first, then check the wiring and connections between the battery and switch and between the switch and wiper motor. If the wiper motor itself is defective, a new or reconditioned unit should be fitted. **FIG 11:10** shows the layout of the windscreen wiper mechanism.

Wiper blade removal:

Lift the wiper arm clear of the windscreen, then pivot the wiper blade around its connection point and pull downwards towards the arm pivot. Refit in the reverse order.

Wiper arm removal:

Make sure that the wiper motor is in the parked position. Refer to **FIG 11:10**. Lift the cover then remove nut 3 and pull the wiper arm from the splined spindle. To refit, push the arm back on to the spindle and tighten the

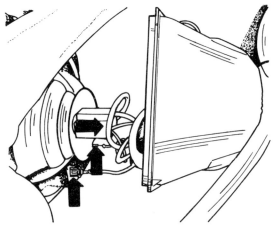

FIG 11:15   Headlamp wiring connections

nut to 5Nm (3.5lb ft). Wiper arms should be fitted so that, with the wiper mechanism in the parked position, the wiper blades are approximately 20mm (0.8in) from the windscreen lower surround. Check the action of the wipers and reposition the arm on the spindle if the wiper blade contacts the windscreen surround at either end of its travel.

Removing wiper mechanism:

Disconnect the battery and remove the windscreen wiper arms from the spindles. Remove spindle base nuts 4 and washers (see FIG 11:10). Remove the lower mounting screw from the wiper motor bracket. Disconnect the wiper motor electrical wiring, then remove the wiper and linkage assembly from the car.

Refitting:

This is a reversal of the removal procedure. Lightly lubricate the bearing points in the operating linkage. Make sure that the wiper crank is in the parked position before attaching the connecting rods (see FIG 11:11).

11:7 Instrument panel
Removal:

Disconnect the battery earth cable. Disconnect the speedometer cable at the transmission. Pull down the panel cover in the lefthand shelf, then press the upper cover upwards until the instrument panel is released (see FIG 11:12). Move the instrument panel towards the steering wheel, then disconnect the speedometer cable from the rear of the speedometer and disconnect the wiring connections from the rear of the unit. The individual instruments, bulbs and the printed circuit board can be removed as shown in FIG 11:13.

Refitting:

This is a reversal of the removal procedure. On completion, check for correct operation of all instruments and lights.

11:8 Headlamps
Bulb renewal:

Headlamp bulbs are accessible from the inside of the engine compartment. Refer to FIG 11:14. Turn cap 8 anticlockwise and pull back for access to the rear of the headlamp unit. Pull off the three-way plug, parking light bulb connector and earth lead, as shown by the arrows in FIG 11:15. Refer to FIG 11:14 and remove rubber cover 7. Turn the retaining ring anticlockwise to remove, then detach the headlamp bulb.

Avoid touching the glass part of the new bulb with the fingers, as this can leave grease marks which darken in use. To prevent this happening, hold the bulb with a piece of clean tissue paper. Install the new bulb, then refit the remaining components in the reverse order of removal.

Headlamp beam setting:

The headlamp beam angles are adjusted by means of the two screws shown at 2 in FIG 11:14. These screws are accessible through the radiator grill slots at the front of the car.

Headlamp main beams should be set so that, when the car is normally loaded the main beams are parallel to each other and to the road. The dipped beams should be set so that they provide a good spread of light to the front and nearside of the car without dazzling oncoming drivers. Accurate beam setting is best left to a service station having special optical equipment.

11:9 Lighting circuits
Lamps give insufficient light:

Refer to Section 11:2 and check the condition of the battery, recharging it if necessary. Check the setting of the headlamps as described in Section 11:8. Make sure that lamp lenses are clean and renew any lamp units or bulbs which have darkened with age.

Bulbs burn out frequently:

Have the alternator regulator setting checked by a service station.

Lamps light when switched on but gradually fade:

Refer to Section 12:2 and check the battery, as it is not capable of supplying current for any length of time. If the fault persists, the alternator should be checked as described in Section 11:3.

Lamp brilliance varies with the speed of the car:

Check the condition of the battery and its connections. Make sure that the connections are clean and tight and renew any faulty cables.

11:10 Fault diagnosis
(a) Battery discharged

1 Terminal connections loose or dirty
2 Shorts in lighting circuits
3 Alternator not charging
4 Regulator faulty
5 Battery internally defective

(b) Insufficient charge rate

1 Check 1 and 4 in (a)
2 Drive belt slipping
3 Alternator diodes defective

(c) Battery will not hold charge

1 Low electrolyte level
2 Battery plates sulphated
3 Electrolyte leakage from cracked case
4 Battery plate separators defective

(d) Battery overcharged

1 Regulator faulty

(e) Alternator output low or nil

1 Drive belt broken or slipping
2 Regulator faulty
3 Brushes sticking, springs weak or broken
4 Defective internal windings
5 Defective diode(s)

(f) Starter motor lacks power or will not turn

1 Battery discharged, loose cable connections
2 Starter switch or solenoid faulty
3 Brushes worn or sticking, leads detached or shorting
4 Commutator dirty or worn
5 Starter shaft bent
6 Engine abnormally stiff, perhaps due to rebore

(g) Starter runs but will not turn engine

1 Pinion engagement mechanism faulty
2 Broken teeth on pinion or flywheel gears

(h) Noisy starter when engine is running

1 Pinion return mechanism faulty

(j) Starter motor inoperative

1 Check 1 and 4 in (f)
2 Armature or field coils faulty
3 Solenoid faulty

(k) Starter motor rough or noisy

1 Mounting bolts loose
2 Pinion engagement mechanism faulty
3 Damaged pinion or flywheel teeth

(l) Lamps inoperative or erratic

1 Battery low, bulbs burned out
2 Faulty earthing of lamps or battery
3 Lighting switch faulty, loose or broken connections

(m) Wiper motor sluggish, taking high current

1 Wiper motor defective internally
2 Lack of lubrication
3 Linkage worn or binding
4 Wiper motor fixing loose

(n) Wiper motor runs but does not drive arms

1 Wiper linkage faulty
2 Wiper transmission components worn

(o) Gauges do not work

1 Check wiring for continuity
2 Check instruments and transmitters for continuity

NOTES

CHAPTER 12

THE BODYWORK

12:1 Bodywork finish

Large scale repairs to body panels are best left to expert panel beaters. Even small dents can be tricky, as too much hammering will stretch the metal and make things worse instead of better. If panel beating is to be attempted, use a dolly on the opposite side of the panel. The head of a large hammer will suffice for small dents, but for large dents a heavy block of metal will be necessary. Use light hammer blows to reshape the panel, pressing the dolly against the opposite side of the panel to absorb the blows. If this method is used to reduce the depth of dents, final smoothing with a suitable filler will be easier, although it may be better to avoid hammering minor dents and just use the filler.

Clean the area to be filled, making sure that it is free from paint, rust and grease, then roughen the area with emerycloth or a file to ensure a good bond. Use a proprietary glassfibre filler paste mixed according to the instructions and press it into the dent with a putty knife. Allow the filler to stand proud of the surrounding area to allow for rubbing down after hardening. Use a file and emerycloth or a disc sander to blend the repaired area to the surrounding bodywork, using finer grade abrasives as

the work nears completion. Apply a coat of primer surfacer and when it is dry, rub down with 'Wet-or-Dry' paper lubricated with soapy water, finishing with 400 grade. Apply more primer and repeat the operation until the surface is perfectly smooth. Take time in achieving the best finish possible at this stage as it will control the final effect.

The touching-up of paintwork can be carried out with self-spraying cans of paint, these being available in a wide range of colours. Use a piece of newspaper or board as a test panel to practice on first, so that the action of the spray will be familiar when it is used on the panel. Before spraying the panel, remove all traces of wax polish. Mask off large areas such as windows with newspaper and masking tape. Small areas such as trim strips or door handles can be wrapped with masking tape or carefully coated with grease or petroleum jelly. Apply the touching-up paint, spraying with short bursts and keeping the spray moving. Do not attempt to cover the area in one coat, applying several successive coats with a few minutes drying time between each. If too much paint is applied at one time, runs will develop. If so, do not try to remove the run by wiping but wait until it is dry and rub down as before.

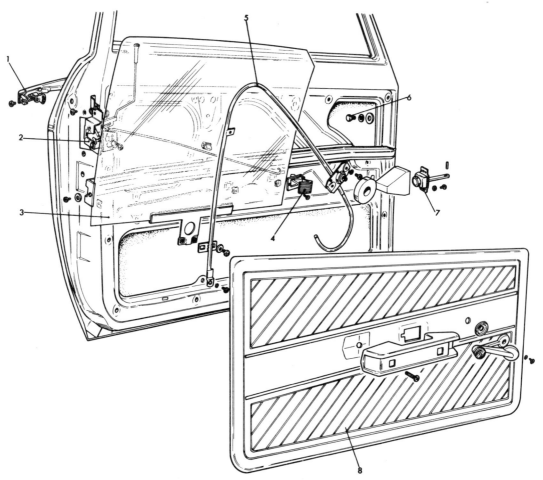

FIG 12:1 Front door components

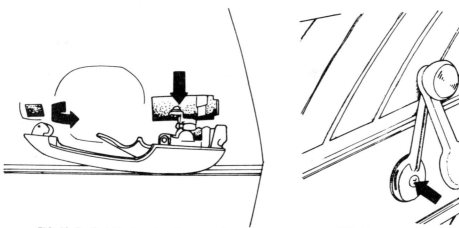

FIG 12:2 Outside door handle removal   **FIG 12:3 Regulator handle removal**

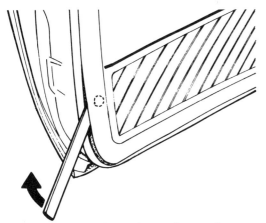

FIG 12:4 Door trim panel removal

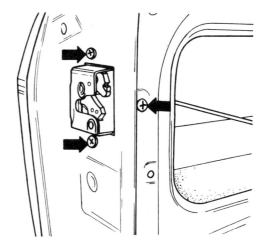

FIG 12:5 Door lock attachment screws

After the final coat has been applied, allow a few hours of drying time before blending the new finish to the old with fine cutting compound and a cloth, buffing with a light, circular motion. Leave the paint to harden for a period of weeks rather than days before applying wax polish.

12:2 Maintenance

Regular washing and waxing not only makes the car look better but it also preserves the finish. Washing removes the industrial grime which would otherwise etch and damage the paintwork, while waxing fills the pores and prevents moisture and dirt from creeping under the paint to attack the metal. Chrome finish also benefits from regular waxing, for the same reasons.

When washing the car it is equally important to wash the underside. Use a fine spray from a hose to soften salt and mud deposits then remove them with a high pressure jet. This is particularly important after winter, as the salt spread on the roads rapidly corrodes the underside of the car. Wax-based oils and other compounds are available for spraying on the underside of the vehicle to protect it from salt and grit, the best time to apply these being at the beginning of winter. **Care must be taken to protect the brake units and flexible hoses from any underbody treatments.**

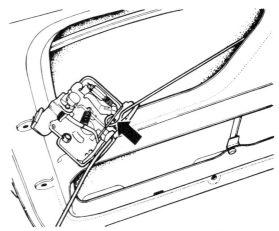

FIG 12:6 Disconnecting remote control linkage

Lubrication:

This should be carried out at regular intervals. The door lock barrels should be lubricated with a little powdered graphite, blown in through the key slot. Door hinges, seat mountings and pivots, and all locks and stays should be lubricated with engine oil. The bonnet catch and luggage compartment lock should be lubricated with petroleum jelly. The seat runners should be lubricated with lithium-based grease. Avoid excessive lubrication which could cause the staining of clothes or upholstery.

12:3 Door components

FIG 12:1 shows front door internal components.

Dismantling:

Remove the outside door handle attachment screw, which is located at the edge of the door. Slide the outside

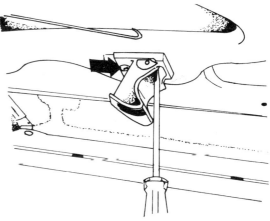

FIG 12:7 Remote control handle removal

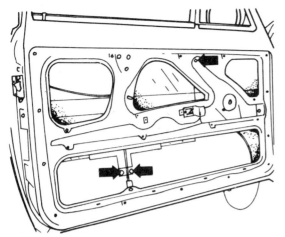

FIG 12:8   Detaching door window from regulator

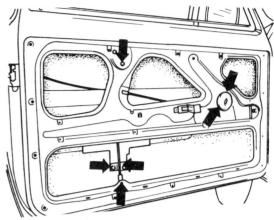

FIG 12:11   Regulator mechanism removal

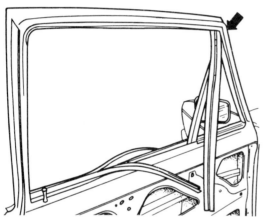

FIG 12:9   Removing window recess seal

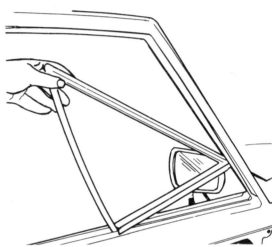

FIG 12:12   Quarter window removal

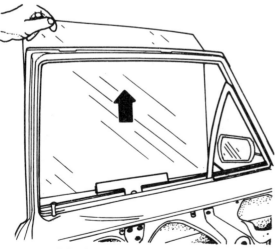

FIG 12:10   Door window removal

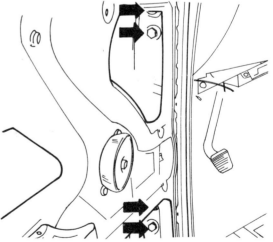

FIG 12:13   Door hinge attachment screws

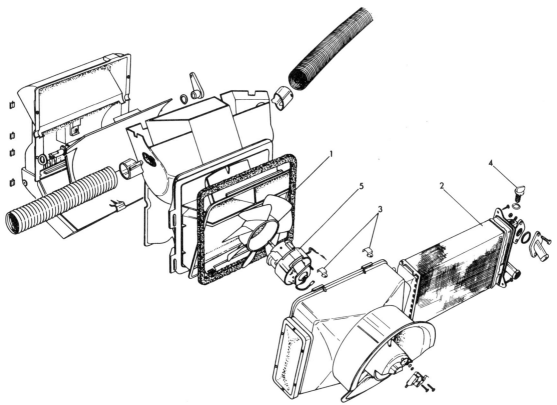

FIG 12:14   Heater components

Key to Fig 12:14   1 Gasket   2 Heater radiator   3 Spring clips   4 Bleed screw   5 Heater blower motor

door handle forwards to disconnect its front end as shown in **FIG 12:2**. Disconnect the connecting rod and detach the handle.

Remove the two fixing screws and detach the armrest. Slide the plastic cover to one side, then remove the single screw and detach the regulator handle as shown in **FIG 12:3**. Using a suitable flat-bladed tool as shown in **FIG 12:4**, carefully lever out the retaining clips and detach the door trim panel.

Remove the three screws arrowed in **FIG 12:5** and detach the door lock assembly, then disconnect the remote control linkage at the point arrowed in **FIG 12:6**. Remove the remote control handle as shown in **FIG 12:7**. Temporarily refit the regulator handle and lower the door window. Detach the door window from the regulator and loosen the window guide rails (see **FIG 12:8**). Unscrew the upper window guide and remove the window recess seal as shown in **FIG 12:9**. Lift the door window upwards and outwards to remove from the door panel, as shown in **FIG 12:10**. Remove the screws arrowed in **FIG 12:11** and detach the window regulator mechanism.

Reassembly:

This is a reversal of the dismantling procedure. Lightly lubricate the window regulator mechanism. Before refitting the trim pad, make sure that the door window can be wound fully from the lower to upper

position, realigning the guide rails if necessary. Check the operation of the door lock from both inside and outside controls before shutting the door.

Quarter window removal:

Remove armrest, regulator handle, trim panel and door window as described previously. The quarter window can then be pulled from position as shown in **FIG 12:12**. Refitting is a reversal of the removal procedure.

Exterior rear view mirror removal:

The exterior rear view mirror is attached by two screws which are accessible after levering out the plastic cover on the mounting.

Door assembly removal:

Remove armrest, regulator handle and trim panel as described previously. Using a suitable punch, drive the dowel pin from the door check strap shown at 7 in **FIG 12:1**. Have an assistant steady the door panel while the hinge attachment bolts arrowed in **FIG 12:13** are removed, then lift off the door assembly complete.

Refitting is a reversal of the removal procedure, making sure that the door fits correctly in the body aperture. Tighten the hinge attachment screws to 22Nm (16lb ft).

12:4 The heater

FIG 12:4 shows heater assembly components.

Heater radiator removal:

Drain the coolant as described in **Chapter 4**, and remove the guard. Lever the connecting rod from the righthand wiper shaft (see **FIG 11:10**). Remove the heater control valve and lay to one side in the water drain tray, then disconnect the lower coolant hose at the heater radiator (see **FIG 12:15**). Remove the clips shown at 3 in **FIG 12:14**, then move the housing and heater radiator assembly forward and carefully remove from the car.

Refitting:

This is a reversal of the removal procedure. Fit a new gasket 1 (see **FIG 12:14**) if the original is not in perfect condition. On completion, refill and bleed the cooling system as described in **Chapter 4**.

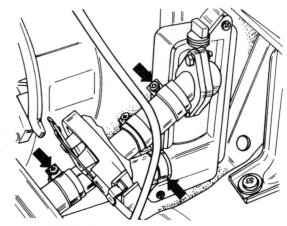

FIG 12:15   Heater control valve removal

APPENDIX

TECHNICAL DATA

HINTS ON MAINTENANCE AND OVERHAUL

GLOSSARY OF TERMS

INDEX

Inches	Decimals	Milli-metres	Inches to Millimetres — Inches	Inches to Millimetres — mm	Millimetres to Inches — mm	Millimetres to Inches — Inches
1/64	.015625	.3969	.001	.0254	.01	.00039
1/32	.03125	.7937	.002	.0508	.02	.00079
3/64	.046875	1.1906	.003	.0762	.03	.00118
1/16	.0625	1.5875	.004	.1016	.04	.00157
5/64	.078125	1.9844	.005	.1270	.05	.00197
3/32	.09375	2.3812	.006	.1524	.06	.00236
7/64	.109375	2.7781	.007	.1778	.07	.00276
1/8	.125	3.1750	.008	.2032	.08	.00315
9/64	.140625	3.5719	.009	.2286	.09	.00354
5/32	.15625	3.9687	.01	.254	.1	.00394
11/64	.171875	4.3656	.02	.508	.2	.00787
3/16	.1875	4.7625	.03	.762	.3	.01181
13/64	.203125	5.1594	.04	1.016	.4	.01575
7/32	.21875	5.5562	.05	1.270	.5	.01969
15/64	.234375	5.9531	.06	1.524	.6	.02362
1/4	.25	6.3500	.07	1.778	.7	.02756
17/64	.265625	6.7469	.08	2.032	.8	.03150
9/32	.28125	7.1437	.09	2.286	.9	.03543
19/64	.296875	7.5406	.1	2.54	1	.03937
5/16	.3125	7.9375	.2	5.08	2	.07874
21/64	.328125	8.3344	.3	7.62	3	.11811
11/32	.34375	8.7312	.4	10.16	4	.15748
23/64	.359375	9.1281	.5	12.70	5	.19685
3/8	.375	9.5250	.6	15.24	6	.23622
25/64	.390625	9.9219	.7	17.78	7	.27559
13/32	.40625	10.3187	.8	20.32	8	.31496
27/64	.421875	10.7156	.9	22.86	9	.35433
7/16	.4375	11.1125	1	25.4	10	.39370
29/64	.453125	11.5094	2	50.8	11	.43307
15/32	.46875	11.9062	3	76.2	12	.47244
31/64	.484375	12.3031	4	101.6	13	.51181
1/2	.5	12.7000	5	127.0	14	.55118
33/64	.515625	13.0969	6	152.4	15	.59055
17/32	.53125	13.4937	7	177.8	16	.62992
35/64	.546875	13.8906	8	203.2	17	.66929
9/16	.5625	14.2875	9	228.6	18	.70866
37/64	.578125	14.6844	10	254.0	19	.74803
19/32	.59375	15.0812	11	279.4	20	.78740
39/64	.609375	15.4781	12	304.8	21	.82677
5/8	.625	15.8750	13	330.2	22	.86614
41/64	.640625	16.2719	14	355.6	23	.90551
21/32	.65625	16.6687	15	381.0	24	.94488
43/64	.671875	17.0656	16	406.4	25	.98425
11/16	.6875	17.4625	17	431.8	26	1.02362
45/64	.703125	17.8594	18	457.2	27	1.06299
23/32	.71875	18.2562	19	482.6	28	1.10236
47/64	.734375	18.6531	20	508.0	29	1.14173
3/4	.75	19.0500	21	533.4	30	1.18110
49/64	.765625	19.4469	22	558.8	31	1.22047
25/32	.78125	19.8437	23	584.2	32	1.25984
51/64	.796875	20.2406	24	609.6	33	1.29921
13/16	.8125	20.6375	25	635.0	34	1.33858
53/64	.828125	21.0344	26	660.4	35	1.37795
27/32	.84375	21.4312	27	685.8	36	1.41732
55/64	.859375	21.8281	28	711.2	37	1.4567
7/8	.875	22.2250	29	736.6	38	1.4961
57/64	.890625	22.6219	30	762.0	39	1.5354
29/32	.90625	23.0187	31	787.4	40	1.5748
59/64	.921875	23.4156	32	812.8	41	1.6142
15/16	.9375	23.8125	33	838.2	42	1.6535
61/64	.953125	24.2094	34	863.6	43	1.6929
31/32	.96875	24.6062	35	889.0	44	1.7323
63/64	.984375	25.0031	36	914.4	45	1.7717

UNITS	Pints to Litres	Gallons to Litres	Litres to Pints	Litres to Gallons	Miles to Kilometres	Kilometres to Miles	Lbs. per sq. In. to Kg. per sq. Cm.	Kg. per sq. Cm. to Lbs. per sq. In.
1	.57	4.55	1.76	.22	1.61	.62	.07	14.22
2	1.14	9.09	3.52	.44	3.22	1.24	.14	28.50
3	1.70	13.64	5.28	.66	4.83	1.86	.21	42.67
4	2.27	18.18	7.04	.88	6.44	2.49	.28	56.89
5	2.84	22.73	8.80	1.10	8.05	3.11	.35	71.12
6	3.41	27.28	10.56	1.32	9.66	3.73	.42	85.34
7	3.98	31.82	12.32	1.54	11.27	4.35	.49	99.56
8	4.55	36.37	14.08	1.76	12.88	4.97	.56	113.79
9		40.91	15.84	1.98	14.48	5.59	.63	128.00
10		45.46	17.60	2.20	16.09	6.21	.70	142.23
20				4.40	32.19	12.43	1.41	284.47
30				6.60	48.28	18.64	2.11	426.70
40				8.80	64.37	24.85		
50					80.47	31.07		
60					96.56	37.28		
70					112.65	43.50		
80					128.75	49.71		
90					144.84	55.92		
100					160.93	62.14		

UNITS	Lb ft to kgm	Kgm to lb ft	UNITS	Lb ft to kgm	Kgm to lb ft
1	.138	7.233	7	.967	50.631
2	.276	14.466	8	1.106	57.864
3	.414	21.699	9	1.244	65.097
4	.553	28.932	10	1.382	72.330
5	.691	36.165	20	2.765	144.660
6	.829	43.398	30	4.147	216.990

TECHNICAL DATA

Dimensions are in millimetres unless otherwise stated

ENGINE

	900cc	1100cc
Bore and stroke	69.5 × 59.0	69.5 × 72.0
Capacity	895cc	1093cc
Compression ratio	8.2:1	8.2:1
Firing order	1–3–4–2	1–3–4–2

Pistons:

Clearance in bore	0.02 to 0.04
Wear limit	0.06

Piston ring side clearance:

Top ring	0.02 to 0.05
Centre ring	0.02 to 0.05
Oil control ring	0.02 to 0.05

Piston ring end gap:

Top ring	0.30 to 0.45
Centre ring	0.30 to 0.45
Oil control ring	0.25 to 0.40

Connecting rod:

Small-end diameter	20.012 to 20.018
Gudgeon pin diameter	19.997 to 20.001
Clearance in small-end	0.01 to 0.02

Crankshaft:

Main journal diameter	53.95 to 53.97
Main bearing clearance	0.036 to 0.095
Wear limit	0.105
Big-end journal diameter	41.95 to 41.97
Big-end bearing clearance	0.020 to 0.076
Wear limit	0.095
Crankshaft end float	0.07 to 0.18
Wear limit	0.20

Cylinder head and valves:

Head seating surface distortion	0.10 maximum

Valve seat width:

Inlet	2.0
Exhaust	2.4
Seat angle, inlet and exhaust	45°

Valve guide inside diameter:

Inlet and exhaust	8.013 to 8.035

Valve stem:

Inlet	7.97
Exhaust	7.95

Stem to guide clearance:

Inlet	0.35
Wear limit	1.0
Exhaust	0.45
Wear limit	1.3

Camshaft:

Journal to bearing clearance	0.050 to 0.114
Wear limit	0.15
Runout at centre bearing	0.02 maximum

Oil pump:

Housing to gear clearance	..	..	..	0.03 to 0.06
Backlash between gears	..	..	..	Zero to 0.13
Pressure relief valve opens at	..	..	..	2.2 to 3.2 bar (31.3 to 45.5lb/sq in)

FUEL SYSTEM

					900cc	1100cc
Carburetter	..	..	..	..	Solex 31 PICT-5	
Jets and settings:					*900cc*	*1100cc*
Venturi	..	..	..	..	23	25.5
Main jet	..	..	..	..	X.115	X.127.5
Air correction jet	..	..	..	..	110.Z	100.Z
Pilot jet	..	..	..	..	50	50
Pilot air jet	..	..	..	..	100	100
Auxiliary jet	..	..	..	..	140	140
Fuel enrichment	..	..	..	..	85/85	65/65
Injection capacity per stroke	..	..	..	0.75 to 1.05cc	0.75 to 1.05cc
Float needle valve	..	..	..	..	1.5	1.5
Needle valve washer	..	..	..	..	2.0	2.0
Throttle valve gap	..	..	..	..	0.8 to 0.9	0.65 to 0.75
Fuel octane requirement	..	..	..	..	91 RON	91 RON
Idling speed	..	..	..	..	900 to 1000rev/min	
CO value	..	..	..	..	2.0 to 3.0% by volume	

IGNITION SYSTEM

Distributor:

Contact breaker gap	..	..	..	0.4 (0.016in)
Static ignition timing	..	..	..	10° BTDC
Dwell angle	..	..	..	44 to 50°

Sparking plugs:

Type	..	..	..	Bosch W175T30, Beru 175/14/3A, Champion N7Y
Plug gap	..	..	..	0.7 (.027in)

COOLING SYSTEM

Thermostat:

Starts to open at	..	..	..	85°C (185°F)
Fully open at	..	..	..	100°C (212°F)

Radiator cap:

High pressure valve opens at	..	..	0.90 to 1.15 bar (12.8 to 16.4lb/sq in)

Cooling fan:

Thermal switch on at	..	..	..	90 to 95°C (194 to 203°F)
Thermal switch off at	..	..	..	85 to 90°C (185 to 194°F)

CLUTCH

Clutch disc runout	..	..	..	0.4 maximum at 175 diameter
Pedal free play	..	..	..	15

TRANSMISSION

Gear ratios:

First	..	..	..	..	3.454:1
Second	..	..	..	..	2.050:1
Third	..	..	..	..	1.347:1
Top	..	..	..	..	0.963:1
Reverse	..	..	..	..	3.384:1
Final drive	..	..	..	..	4.571:1 (900cc), 4.267:1 (1100cc)

FRONT AXLE

Front wheel toe-in	$0° \pm 10'$
Camber angle	$+ 20' \pm 30'$
Maximum permissible difference between sides ..	$30'$
Castor angle, each wheel	$20° 20' \pm 30'$

REAR AXLE

Rear wheel toe-in	$0° + 30'/- 10'$
Camber angle	$- 30' \pm 35'$
Maximum permissible difference between sides ..	$35'$

BRAKES

Front:

Disc diameter	239
Disc thickness	8.0
Minimum thickness	7.0

Rear:

Drum diameter	180
Maximum diameter	181

ELECTRICAL

System polarity	Negative earth
Battery capacity	36 amp/hr
Starter motor	0.51Kw/0.7HP
Alternator	35A standard, 55A optional equipment

CAPACITIES

Engine sump only	3.0 litres (5.2 pints)
Sump and oil filter	3.25 litres (5.7 pints)
Gearbox	2.35 litres (4.1 pints)
Cooling system	6.5 litres (11.6 pints)
Fuel tank	36 litres (8 gallons)

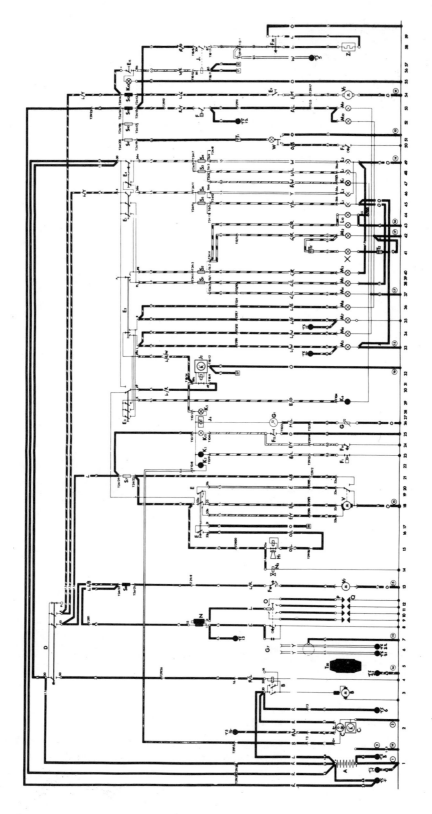

FIG 13:1 Basic current flow diagram

Key to Fig 13:1 *Numbers on right relate to those on diagram base line to locate items*

Code	Description	Numbers
A	Battery	1
B	Starter	3, 4
C	Generator	2
C1	Voltage regulator	2
D	Ignition-starter switch	4, 8, 10, 12
E	Wiper switch	16–20
E1	Lighting switch	44–47
E2	Turn signal switch	34–39
E3	Emergency light switch	27–30
E4	Dip and flasher switch	47–49
E9	Fresh air motor switch	54
E15	Heated rear window switch	55–56
F	Brake light switch	53
F1	Oil pressure switch	23
F2	Door contact switch, left	50
F12	Contact for choke warning lamp	
F14	Temperature warning switch	25
F18	Radiator fan thermoswitch	13
F28	Rear window contact (in tailgate)	58, 59
G	Fuel gauge sender	26
G1	Fuel gauge	26
G7	Connection for TDC sensor	6, 7
H1	Horn	15
J2	Emergency light relay	31, 32
J6	Voltage stabiliser	26
J9	Heated rear window relay	56, 58
K1	High beam warning lamp	47
K2	Generator warning lamp	22
K3	Oil pressure warning lamp	23
K5	Turn signal warning lamp	28
K6	Emergency light warning lamp	29
K10	Rear window warning lamp	55
K15	Choke and coolant temperature warning lamp	
L1	Headlight, left	45, 48
L2	Headlight, right	46, 49
L10	Instrument panel light	43, 44
M1	Side light, left	38
M2	Side light, right	42
M3	Tail light, right	40
M4	Tail light, left	37
M5	Turn signal front left	33
M6	Turn signal rear left	34
M7	Turn signal front right	35
M8	Turn signal rear right	36
M9	Brake light left	53
M10	Brake light right	52
N	Ignition coil	8
N3	Cut-off valve solenoid	14
O	Distributor	26
P	Plug connectors	8–12
Q	Spark plugs	9–12
S1 to S12	Fuses in fuse box	
T1	Flat connector	
T2	Connector, 2-pin	
T6	Connector, 6-pin on fuse box	
T10	Connector, 12-pin on dash insert	
T12	Connector, 12-pin dash–tail light wiring, under dash on left	
T20	Test socket	5
T24	Connector, 24-pin on fuse box	
T29	Connector, 29-pin dash–engine wiring, on fuse box	
TS5, TS12 etc.	Numbered terminals in diagnostic test socket T20	
V	Wiper motor	19
V2	Fresh air fan motor	54
V7	Radiator fan motor	13
W	Interior light	51
X	Number plate light	41
Z1	Rear window heater	58

Circled numbers:

1	Earth strap, battery to body
2	Earth strap, generator to engine
3	Earth strap, engine to body
14	Earth point, in plenum chamber
15	Earth point, in plenum chamber
16	Earth point, on left under dash
17	Earth point, on left tail light

Wiring colour code   **B** Blue   **E** Green   **G** Grey   **L** Black   **M** Mauve   **O** Brown   **R** Red   **W** White   **Y** Yellow

When wires have two colour code letters the first denotes the main colour, the second the stripe. Numbers in wires (eg. 2.5, 0.5) indicate cross-sectional area of wire in sq mm

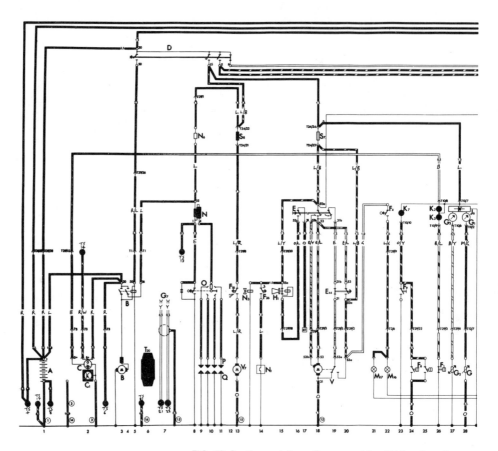

FIG 13:2 Current flow diagram with additional equipment

Key to Fig 13:2 *Numbers on right relate to those on diagram base line to locate items*

A	Battery	1
B	Starter	3–5
C	Generator	2
C1	Voltage regulator	2
D	Ignition/starter switch	5–12
F	Wiper switch	16–19
E1	Lighting switch	46–48
E2	Turn signal switch	35–42
E3	Emergency light switch	29–34
E4	Dip and flasher switch	48–51
E9	Fresh air motor switch	59
E15	Heated rear window switch	60–62
E44	Wash/wipe switch	19–20
F	Brake light switch	58
F1	Oil pressure switch	26
F2	Door contact switch, left	54
F3	Door contact switch, right	53
F4	Reversing light switch	22
F6	Brake system warning switch	24, 25
F9	Handbrake warning switch	23
F18	Coolant fan thermoswitch	13

F26	Automatic choke thermoswitch	14
F28	Heated rear window contact (in tailgate)	63, 64
G	Fuel gauge sender	28
G1	Fuel gauge	28
G2	Temperature gauge sender	27
G3	Temperature gauge	27
G7	TDC sensor	7
H1	Horn	15
J2	Emergency light/turn signal relay	33, 34
J6	Voltage stabiliser	27, 28
J9	Heated rear window relay	62, 63
K1	High beam warning lamp	49
K2	Generator warning lamp	26
K3	Oil pressure warning lamp	26
K5	Turn signal warning lamp	30
K6	Emergency light warning lamp	31

K7	Dual circuit and handbrake warning lamp	23
K10	Heated rear window warning lamp	60
L1	Headlight bulb, left	47, 50
L2	Headlight bulb, right	48, 51
L10	Instrument panel light	45, 46
M1	Side light, right	40
M2	Tail light, right	44
M3	Side light, right	42
M4	Tail light, left	39
M5	Turn signal front left	35
M6	Turn signal rear left	36
M7	Turn signal front right	37
M8	Turn signal rear right	38
M9	Brake light, left	58
M10	Brake light, right	57
M16	Reversing light, left	22
M17	Reversing light, right	21
N	Ignition coil	8
N1	Automatic choke	14
N3	Cut-off valve solenoid	13, 14
N6	Series resistance	8
O	Distributor	9–11
P	Plug connector	9–11
Q	Spark plugs	9–11

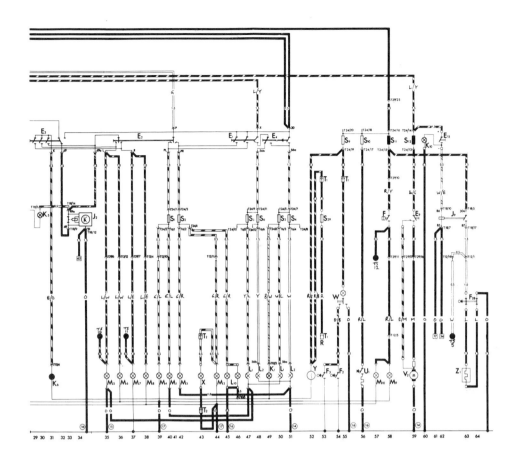

R	Radio connection	53
S1 to		
S12	Fuses in fuse box	
S29	Radio fuse	53
T1	Connector, single	
T2	Connector, 2-pin (on luggage compartment rear panel)	
T3	Connector, 3-pin (in engine compartment on partition)	
T6	Connector, 6-pin (on fuse box, plenum chamber side)	
T12	Connector, 12-pin (under dash on left)	

T18	Relay adaptor, 18-pin (under dash on left)	
T20	Test socket	
T24	Connector, 24-pin (on fuse box)	
T29	Connector 29-pin (on fuse box)	
TS5, TS12 etc	Numbered terminals in diagnostic test socket T20	
U1	Cigarette lighter	56
V	Wiper motor	18
V2	Fresh air motor	59
V7	Radiator fan motor	13
W	Interior light	55
X	Number plate light	43

| Y | Clock | 52 |
| Z1 | Heated rear window | 63 |

Circled numbers:

1	Earth strap, battery to body
2	Earth strap, generator to engine
3	Earth strap, engine to body
14	Earth point, in plenum chamber
15	Earth point, in plenum chamber
16	Earth point on left under dash
17	Earth point on left tail light

Diagram includes market variations and optional equipment; not all items are fitted to all models

Wiring colour code   **B** Blue   **E** Green   **G** Grey   **L** Black   **M** Mauve   **O** Brown   **R** Red   **W** White   **Y** Yellow

When wires have two colour code letters the first denotes the main colour, the second the stripe. Numbers in wires (eg, 2.5, 0.5) indicate cross-sectional area of wire in sq mm

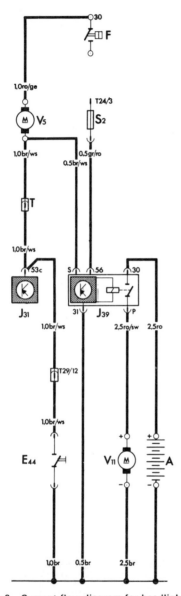

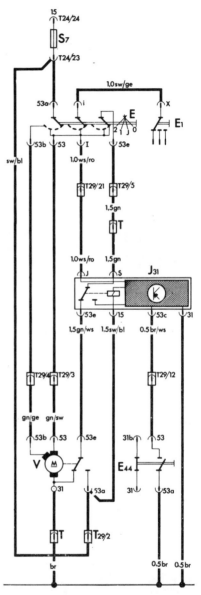

FIG 13:3 Current flow diagram for headlight washer

Key to Fig 13:3   A Battery   E44 Switch (foot switch without pump)   F Brake light switch   J31 Relay for intermittent wiper and wash/wipe   J39 Relay for headlight washer S2 Second fuse in fuse box   T Connector   V5 Windscreen washer pump   V11 Headlight washer pump

Wiring colour code   br Brown   **ge** Yellow   **gr** Green **ro** Red   **sw** Black   **ws** white

Number preceding colour code indicates cross-sectional area of wire in sq mm

FIG 13:4 Current flow diagram for intermittent wipe and wash/wipe system

Key to Fig 13:4   E Wiper switch   E1 Lighting switch E44 Switch and foot pump   J31 Relay for intermittent wipe and wash/wipe   S7 Fuse in fuse box   V Wiper motor

Wiring colour code   br Brown   **ge** Yellow   **gr** Green **ro** Red   **sw** Black   **ws** White

Number preceding colour code indicates cross-sectional area of wire in sq mm

HINTS ON MAINTENANCE AND OVERHAUL

There are few things more rewarding than the restoration of a vehicle's original peak of efficiency and smooth performance.

The following notes are intended to help the owner to reach that state of perfection. Providing that he possesses the basic manual skills he should have no difficulty in performing most of the operations detailed in this manual. It must be stressed, however, that where recommended in the manual, highly-skilled operations ought to be entrusted to experts, who have the necessary equipment, to carry out the work satisfactorily.

Quality of workmanship:

The hazardous driving conditions on the roads to-day demand that vehicles should be as nearly perfect, mechanically, as possible. It is therefore most important that amateur work be carried out with care, bearing in mind the often inadequate working conditions, and also the inferior tools which may have to be used. It is easy to counsel perfection in all things, and we recognize that it may be setting an impossibly high standard. We do, however, suggest that every care should be taken to ensure that a vehicle is as safe to take on the road as it is humanly possible to make it.

Safe working conditions:

Even though a vehicle may be stationary, it is still potentially dangerous if certain sensible precautions are not taken when working on it while it is supported on jacks or blocks. It is indeed preferable not to use jacks alone, but to supplement them with carefully placed blocks, so that there will be plenty of support if the car rolls off the jacks during a strenuous manoeuvre. Axle stands are an excellent way of providing a rigid base which is not readily disturbed. Piles of bricks are a dangerous substitute. Be careful not to get under heavy loads on lifting tackle, the load could fall. It is preferable not to work alone when lifting an engine, or when working underneath a vehicle which is supported well off the ground. To be trapped, particularly under the vehicle, may have unpleasant results if help is not quickly forthcoming. Make some provision, however humble, to deal with fires. Always disconnect a battery if there is a likelihood of electrical shorts. These may start a fire if there is leaking fuel about. This applies particularly to leads which can carry a heavy current, like those in the starter circuit. While on the subject of electricity, we must also stress the danger of using·equipment which is run off the mains and which has no earth or has faulty wiring or connections. So many workshops have damp floors, and electrical shocks are of such a nature that it is sometimes impossible to let go of a live lead or piece of equipment due to the muscular spasms which take place.

Work demanding special care:

This involves the servicing of braking, steering and suspension systems. On the road, failure of the braking system may be disastrous. Make quite sure that there can be no possibility of failure through the bursting of rusty brake pipes or rotten hoses, nor to a sudden loss of pressure due to defective seals or valves.

Problems:

The chief problems which may face an operator are:
1 External dirt.
2 Difficulty in undoing tight fixings
3 Dismantling unfamiliar mechanisms.
4 Deciding in what respect parts are defective.
5 Confusion about the correct order for reassembly.
6 Adjusting running clearances.
7 Road testing.
8 Final tuning.

Practical suggestions to solve the problems:

1 Preliminary cleaning of large parts—engines, transmissions, steering, suspensions, etc.,—should be carried out before removal from the car. Where road dirt and mud alone are present, wash clean with a high-pressure water jet, brushing to remove stubborn adhesions, and allow to drain and dry. Where oil or grease is also present, wash down with a proprietary compound (Gunk, Teepol etc.,) applying with a stiff brush—an old paint brush is suitable—into all crevices. Cover the distributor and ignition coils with a polythene bag and then apply a strong water jet to clear the loosened deposits. Allow to drain and dry. The assemblies will then be sufficiently clean to remove and transfer to the bench for the next stage.

On the bench, further cleaning can be carried out, first wiping the parts as free as possible from grease with old newspaper. Avoid using rag or cotton waste which can leave clogging fibres behind. Any remaining grease can be removed with a brush dipped in paraffin. If necessary, traces of paraffin can be removed by carbon tetrachloride. Avoid using paraffin or petrol in large quantities for cleaning in enclosed areas, such as garages, on account of the high fire risk.

When all exteriors have been cleaned, and not before, dismantling can be commenced. This ensures that dirt will not enter into interiors and orifices revealed by dismantling. In the next phases, where components have to be cleaned, use carbon tetrachloride in preference to petrol and keep the containers covered except when in use. After the components have been cleaned, plug small holes with tapered hard wood plugs cut to size and blank off larger orifices with grease-proof paper and masking tape. Do not use soft wood plugs or matchsticks as they may break.

2 It is not advisable to hammer on the end of a screw thread, but if it must be done, first screw on a nut to protect the thread, and use a lead hammer. This applies particularly to the removal of tapered cotters. Nuts and bolts seem to 'grow' together, especially in exhaust systems. If penetrating oil does not work, try the judicious application of heat, but be careful of starting a fire. Asbestos sheet or cloth is useful to isolate heat.

Tight bushes or pieces of tail-pipe rusted into a silencer can be removed by splitting them with an open-ended hacksaw. Tight screws can sometimes be started by a tap from a hammer on the end of a suitable screwdriver. Many tight fittings will yield to the judicious use of a hammer, but it must be a soft-faced hammer if damage is to be avoided, use a heavy block on the opposite side to absorb shock. Any parts of the steering system which have been damaged should be renewed, as attempts to repair them may lead to cracking and subsequent failure, and steering ball joints should be disconnected using a recommended tool to prevent damage.

3 If often happens that an owner is baffled when trying to dismantle an unfamiliar piece of equipment. So many modern devices are pressed together or assembled by spinning-over flanges, that they must be sawn apart. The intention is that the whole assembly must be renewed. However, parts which appear to be in one piece to the naked eye, may reveal close-fitting joint lines when inspected with a magnifying glass, and, this may provide the necessary clue to dismantling. Left-handed screw threads are used where rotational forces would tend to unscrew a righthanded screw thread.

Be very careful when dismantling mechanisms which may come apart suddenly. Work in an enclosed space where the parts will be contained, and drape a piece of cloth over the device if springs are likely to fly in all directions. Mark everything which might be reassembled in the wrong position, scratched symbols may be used on unstressed parts, or a sequence of tiny dots from a centre punch can be useful. Stressed parts should never be scratched or centre-popped as this may lead to cracking under working conditions. Store parts which look alike in the correct order for reassembly. Never rely upon memory to assist in the assembly of complicated mechanisms, especially when they will be dismantled for a long time, but make notes, and drawings to supplement the diagrams in the manual, and put labels on detached wires. Rust stains may indicate unlubricated wear. This can sometimes be seen round the outside edge of a bearing cup in a universal joint. Look for bright rubbing marks on parts which normally should not make heavy contact. These might prove that something is bent or running out of truth. For example, there might be bright marks on one side of a piston, at the top near the ring grooves, and others at the bottom of the skirt on the other side. This could well be the clue to a bent connecting rod. Suspected cracks can be proved by heating the component in a light oil to approximately 100°C, removing, drying off, and dusting with french chalk, if a crack is present the oil retained in the crack will stain the french chalk.

4 In determining wear, and the degree, against the permissible limits set in the manual, accurate measurement can only be achieved by the use of a micrometer. In many cases, the wear is given to the fourth place of decimals; that is in ten-thousandths of an inch. This can be read by the vernier scale on the barrel of a good micrometer. Bore diameters are more difficult to determine. If, however, the matching shaft is accurately measured, the degree of play in the bore can be felt as a guide to its suitability. In other cases, the shank of a twist drill of known diameter is a handy check.

Many methods have been devised for determining the clearance between bearing surfaces. To-day the best and simplest is by the use of Plastigage, obtainable from most garages. A thin plastic thread is laid between the two surfaces and the bearing is tightened, flattening the thread. On removal, the width of the thread is compared with a scale supplied with the thread and the clearance is read off directly. Sometimes joint faces leak persistently, even after gasket renewal. The fault will then be traceable to distortion, dirt or burrs. Studs which are screwed into soft metal frequently raise burrs at the point of entry. A quick cure for this is to chamfer the edge of the hole in the part which fits over the stud.

5 **Always check a replacement part with the original one before it is fitted.**

If parts are not marked, and the order for reassembly is not known, a little detective work will help. Look for marks which are due to wear to see if they can be mated. Joint faces may not be identical due to manufacturing errors, and parts which overlap may be stained, giving a clue to the correct position. Most fixings leave identifying marks especially if they were painted over on assembly. It is then easier to decide whether a nut, for instance, has a plain, a spring, or a shakeproof washer under it. All running surfaces become 'bedded' together after long spells of work and tiny imperfections on one part will be found to have left corresponding marks on the other. This is particularly true of shafts and bearings and even a score on a cylinder wall will show on the piston.

6 Checking end float or rocker clearances by feeler gauge may not always give accurate results because of wear. For instance, the rocker tip which bears on a valve stem may be deeply pitted, in which case the feeler will simply be bridging a depression. Thrust washers may also wear depressions in opposing faces to make accurate measurement difficult. End float is then easier to check by using a dial gauge. It is common practice to adjust end play in bearing assemblies, like front hubs with taper rollers, by doing up the axle nut until the hub becomes stiff to turn and then backing it off a little. Do not use this method with ballbearing hubs as the assembly is often preloaded by tightening the axle nut to its fullest extent. If the splitpin hole will not line up, file the base of the nut a little.

Steering assemblies often wear in the straight-ahead position. If any part is adjusted, make sure that it remains free when moved from lock to lock. Do not be surprised if an assembly like a steering gearbox, which is known to be carefully adjusted outside the car, becomes stiff when it is bolted in place. This will be due to distortion of the case by the pull of the mounting bolts, particularly if the mounting points are not all touching together. This problem may be met in other equipment and is cured by careful attention to the alignment of mounting points.

When a spanner is stamped with a size and A/F it means that the dimension is the width between the jaws and has no connection with ANF, which is the designation for the American National Fine thread. Coarse threads like Whitworth are rarely used on cars to-day except for studs which screw into soft aluminium or cast iron. For this reason it might be found that the top end of a cylinder head stud has a fine thread and the lower end a coarse thread to screw into the cylinder block. If the car has mainly UNF threads then it is likely that any coarse threads will be UNC, which are not the same as Whitworth. Small sizes have the same number of threads in Whitworth and UNC, but in the $\frac{1}{2}$ inch size for example, there are twelve threads to the inch in the former and thirteen in the latter.

7 After a major overhaul, particularly if a great deal of work has been done on the braking, steering and suspension systems, it is advisable to approach the problem of testing with care. If the braking system has been overhauled, apply heavy pressure to the brake pedal and get a second operator to check every possible source of leakage. The brakes may work extremely well, but a leak could cause complete failure after a few miles.

Do not fit the hub caps until every wheel nut has been checked for tightness, and make sure the tyre pressures are correct. Check the levels of coolant, lubricants and hydraulic fluids. Being satisfied that all is well, take the car on the road and test the brakes at once. Check the steering and the action of the handbrake. Do all this at moderate speeds on quiet roads, and make sure there is no other vehicle behind you when you try a rapid stop.

Finally, remember that many parts settle down after a time, so check for tightness of all fixings after the car has been on the road for a hundred miles or so.

8 It is useless to tune an engine which has not reached its normal running temperature. In the same way, the tune of an engine which is stiff after a rebore will be different when the engine is again running free. Remember too, that rocker clearances on pushrod operated valve gear will change when the cylinder head nuts are tightened after an initial period of running with a new head gasket.

Trouble may not always be due to what seems the obvious cause. Ignition, carburation and mechanical condition are interdependent and spitting back through the carburetter, which might be attributed to a weak mixture, can be caused by a sticking inlet valve.

For one final hint on tuning, never adjust more than one thing at a time or it will be impossible to tell which adjustment produced the desired result.

NOTES

GLOSSARY OF TERMS

Allen key   Cranked wrench of hexagonal section for use with socket head screws.

Alternator   Electrical generator producing alternating current. Rectified to direct current for battery charging.

Ambient temperature   Surrounding atmospheric temperature.

Annulus   Used in engineering to indicate the outer ring gear of an epicyclic gear train.

Armature   The shaft carrying the windings, which rotates in the magnetic field of a generator or starter motor. That part of a solenoid or relay which is activated by the magnetic field.

Axial   In line with, or pertaining to, an axis.

Backlash   Play in meshing gears.

Balance lever   A bar where force applied at the centre is equally divided between connections at the ends.

Banjo axle   Axle casing with large diameter housing for the crownwheel and differential.

Bendix pinion   A self-engaging and self-disengaging drive on a starter motor shaft.

Bevel pinion   A conical shaped gearwheel, designed to mesh with a similar gear with an axis usually at 90 deg. to its own.

bhp   Brake horse power, measured on a dynamometer.

bmep   Brake mean effective pressure. Average pressure on a piston during the working stroke.

Brake cylinder   Cylinder with hydraulically operated piston(s) acting on brake shoes or pad(s).

Brake regulator   Control valve fitted in hydraulic braking system which limits brake pressure to rear brakes during heavy braking to prevent rear wheel locking.

Camber   Angle at which a wheel is tilted from the vertical.

Capacitor   Modern term for an electrical condenser. Part of distributor assembly, connected across contact breaker points, acts as an interference suppressor.

Castellated   Top face of a nut, slotted across the flats, to take a locking splitpin.

Castor   Angle at which the kingpin or swivel pin is tilted when viewed from the side.

cc   Cubic centimetres. Engine capacity is arrived at by multiplying the area of the bore in sq cm by the stroke in cm by the number of cylinders.

Clevis   U-shaped forked connector used with a clevis pin, usually at handbrake connections.

Collet   A type of collar, usually split and located in a groove in a shaft, and held in place by a retainer. The arrangement used to retain the spring(s) on a valve stem in most cases.

Commutator   Rotating segmented current distributor between armature windings and brushes in generator or motor.

Compression ratio   The ratio, or quantitative relation, of the total volume (piston at bottom of stroke) to the unswept volume (piston at top of stroke) in an engine cylinder.

Condenser   See capacitor.

Core plug   Plug for blanking off a manufacturing hole in a casting.

Crownwheel   Large bevel gear in rear axle, driven by a bevel pinion attached to the propeller shaft. Sometimes called a 'ring gear'.

'C'-spanner   Like a 'C' with a handle. For use on screwed collars without flats, but with slots or holes.

Damper   Modern term for shock-absorber, used in vehicle suspension systems to damp out spring oscillations.

Depression   The lowering of atmospheric pressure as in the inlet manifold and carburetter.

Dowel   Close tolerance pin, peg, tube, or bolt, which accurately locates mating parts.

Drag link   Rod connecting steering box drop arm (pitman arm) to nearest front wheel steering arm in certain types of steering systems.

Dry liner   Thinwall tube pressed into cylinder bore

Dry sump   Lubrication system where all oil is scavenged from the sump, and returned to a separate tank.

Dynamo   See Generator.

Electrode   Terminal, part of an electrical component, such as the points or 'Electrodes' of a sparking plug.

Electrolyte   In lead-acid car batteries a solution of sulphuric acid and distilled water.

End float   The axial movement between associated parts, end play.

EP   Extreme pressure. In lubricants, special grades for heavily loaded bearing surfaces, such as gear teeth in a gearbox, or crownwheel and pinion in a rear axle.

Fade	Of brakes. Reduced efficiency due to overheating.
Field coils	Windings on the polepieces of motors and generators.
Fillets	Narrow finishing strips usually applied to interior bodywork.
First motion shaft	Input shaft from clutch to gearbox.
Fullflow filter	Filters in which all the oil is pumped to the engine. If the element becomes clogged, a bypass valve operates to pass unfiltered oil to the engine.
FWD	Front wheel drive.
Gear pump	Two meshing gears in a close fitting casing. Oil is carried from the inlet round the outside of both gears in the spaces between the gear teeth and casing to the outlet, the meshing gear teeth prevent oil passing back to the inlet, and the oil is forced through the outlet port.
Generator	Modern term for 'Dynamo'. When rotated produces electrical current.
Grommet	A ring of protective or sealing material. Can be used to protect pipes or leads passing through bulkheads.
Grubscrew	Fully threaded headless screw with screwdriver slot. Used for locking, or alignment purposes.
Gudgeon pin	Shaft which connects a piston to its connecting rod. Sometimes called 'wrist pin', or 'piston pin'.
Halfshaft	One of a pair transmitting drive from the differential.
Helical	In spiral form. The teeth of helical gears are cut at a spiral angle to the side faces of the gearwheel.
Hot spot	Hot area that assists vapourisation of fuel on its way to cylinders. Often provided by close contact between inlet and exhaust manifolds.
HT	High Tension. Applied to electrical current produced by the ignition coil for the sparking plugs.
Hydrometer	A device for checking specific gravity of liquids. Used to check specific gravity of electrolyte.
Hypoid bevel gears	A form of bevel gear used in the rear axle drive gears. The bevel pinion meshes below the centre line of the crownwheel, giving a lower propeller shaft line.
Idler	A device for passing on movement. A free running gear between driving and driven gears. A lever transmitting track rod movement to a side rod in steering gear.
Impeller	A centrifugal pumping element. Used in water pumps to stimulate flow.
Journals	Those parts of a shaft that are in contact with the bearings.
Kingpin	The main vertical pin which carries the front wheel spindle, and permits steering movement. May be called 'steering pin' or 'swivel pin'.
Layshaft	The shaft which carries the laygear in the gearbox. The laygear is driven by the first motion shaft and drives the third motion shaft according to the gear selected. Sometimes called the 'countershaft' or 'second motion shaft.'
lb ft	A measure of twist or torque. A pull of 10 lb at a radius of 1 ft is a torque of 10 lb ft.
lb/sq in	Pounds per square inch.
Little-end	The small, or piston end of a connecting rod. Sometimes called the 'small-end'.
LT	Low Tension. The current output from the battery.
Mandrel	Accurately manufactured bar or rod used for test or centring purposes.
Manifold	A pipe, duct, or chamber, with several branches.
Needle rollers	Bearing rollers with a length many times their diameter.
Oil bath	Reservoir which lubricates parts by immersion. In air filters, a separate oil supply for wetting a wire mesh element to hold the dust.
Oil wetted	In air filters, a wire mesh element lightly oiled to trap and hold airborne dust.
Overlap	Period during which inlet and exhaust valves are open together.
Panhard rod	Bar connected between fixed point on chassis and another on axle to control sideways movement.
Pawl	Pivoted catch which engages in the teeth of a ratchet to permit movement in one direction only.
Peg spanner	Tool with pegs, or pins, to engage in holes or slots in the part to be turned.
Pendant pedals	Pedals with levers that are pivoted at the top end.
Phillips screwdriver	A cross-point screwdriver for use with the cross-slotted heads of Phillips screws.
Pinion	A small gear, usually in relation to another gear.
Piston-type damper	Shock absorber in which damping is controlled by a piston working in a closed oil-filled cylinder.
Preloading	Preset static pressure on ball or roller bearings not due to working loads.
Radial	Radiating from a centre, like the spokes of a wheel.

Radius rod	Pivoted arm confining movement of a part to an arc of fixed radius.
Ratchet	Toothed wheel or rack which can move in one direction only, movement in the other being prevented by a pawl.
Ring gear	A gear tooth ring attached to outer periphery of flywheel. Starter pinion engages with it during starting.
Runout	Amount by which rotating part is out of true.
Semi-floating axle	Outer end of rear axle halfshaft is carried on bearing inside axle casing. Wheel hub is secured to end of shaft.
Servo	A hydraulic or pneumatic system for assisting, or, augmenting a physical effort. See 'Vacuum Servo'.
Setscrew	One which is threaded for the full length of the shank.
Shackle	A coupling link, used in the form of two parallel pins connected by side plates to secure the end of the master suspension spring and absorb the effects of deflection.
Shell bearing	Thinwalled steel shell lined with anti-friction metal. Usually semi-circular and used in pairs for main and big-end bearings.
Shock absorber	See 'Damper'.
Silentbloc	Rubber bush bonded to inner and outer metal sleeves.
Socket-head screw	Screw with hexagonal socket for an Allen key.
Solenoid	A coil of wire creating a magnetic field when electric current passes through it. Used with a soft iron core to operate contacts or a mechanical device.
Spur gear	A gear with teeth cut axially across the periphery.
Stub axle	Short axle fixed at one end only.
Tachometer	An instrument for accurate measurement of rotating speed. Usually indicates in revolutions per minute.

TDC	Top Dead Centre. The highest point reached by a piston in a cylinder, with the crank and connecting rod in line.
Thermostat	Automatic device for regulating temperature. Used in vehicle coolant systems to open a valve which restricts circulation at low temperature.
Third motion shaft	Output shaft of gearbox.
Threequarter floating axle	Outer end of rear axle halfshaft flanged and bolted to wheel hub, which runs on bearing mounted on outside of axle casing. Vehicle weight is not carried by the axle shaft.
Thrust bearing or washer	Used to reduce friction in rotating parts subject to axial loads.
Torque	Turning or twisting effort. See 'lb ft'.
Track rod	The bar(s) across the vehicle which connect the steering arms and maintain the front wheels in their correct alignment.
UJ	Universal joint. A coupling between shafts which permits angular movement.
UNF	Unified National Fine screw thread.
Vacuum servo	Device used in brake system, using difference between atmospheric pressure and inlet manifold depression to operate a piston which acts to augment brake pressure as required. See 'Servo'.
Venturi	A restriction or 'choke' in a tube, as in a carburetter, used to increase velocity to obtain a reduction in pressure.
Vernier	A sliding scale for obtaining fractional readings of the graduations of an adjacent scale.
Welch plug	A domed thin metal disc which is partially flattened to lock in a recess. Used to plug core holes in castings.
Wet liner	Removable cylinder barrel, sealed against coolant leakage, where the coolant is in direct contact with the outer surface.
Wet sump	A reservoir attached to the crankcase to hold the lubricating oil.

NOTES

INDEX

W

NOTES

NOTES

NOTES

NOTES

NOTES